Adventures in Fur, Feathers and Fun

Fly Tying

Adventures in Fur, Feathers and Fun

John F. McKim

Illustrations by the author

MOUNTAIN PRESS PUBLISHING COMPANY
P.O. Box 2399
Missoula, Montana 59806

Eighth Printing
January 1998

Library of Congress Cataloging-in-Publication Data

McKim, John F.
    Fly Tying—.

    Bibliography: p.
    1. Fly tying. I. Title.
SH451.M4   688.7'912   82-2077
ISBN 0-87842-140-8   AACR2

MOUNTAIN PRESS PUBLISHING COMPANY
P.O. Box 2399
Missoula, Montana 59806

To Joanie, my love my wife,
who believed in me before I ever dared.

Foreword

I first met John McKim in 1972 when we became members of the staff of the FFF Bulletin, he as Art Director and Editor of the "Tie Flyer," and I as its Editor. This came about by the decision of the new President of the Federation of Fly Fishermen, Jim Eriser, to change the Bulletin's existing format and increase its importance.

During the four years we worked together on the Bulletin, we shared the proofing and pasteup, deadline pressure and relief, disappointments and triumphs, all of the problems and pleasures that attended the publication of each issue. When John left to enter the commercial field there were a great many members who felt his loss, none more so than I. We had become good friends.

John graduated from U.C.L.A. where he majored in art. Although he studied to become a painter and, under the influence of Stanton MacDonald Wright and others, painted in an abstract manner, this did not affect his ability to draw realistically when the need arose. The fine quality drawings in this volume are proof of that. In my opinion, John is a consummate draughtsman, unsurpassed in pen and ink, a medium particularly well suited to illustrating a book on how to tie flies. As a matter of fact, while working with him on the FFF Bulletin I was continually astounded by his ability to make a finished drawing without so much as a preliminary sketch. Michelangelo is said to have worked that way.

Not all of the book's illustrations are line drawings, of course. Photographs have been included but only where John feels they can best illuminate the subject.

In "Fly Tying...Adventures in Fur, Feathers and Fun" John states that it is a manual for the beginning fly tier. It is all of that. But I have a suspicion that among its readers will be many who are seeking a refresher course in how to tie flies.

J. Stanley Lloyd

Preface

What makes fly tiers so special? Extraordinary talent? Super dexterity? Neither. To learn to tie flies you need just two things: the desire to learn and a willingness to try. There's no mystique to fly tying. That's pure illusion. Suprisingly, it's the rare individual who cannot learn to tie flies. If you can learn to tie a knot, you can learn to tie a fly. The only difference between you and those wizards of the vise who seem able to work magic with bits of feathers and fur is time and practice. They, like you, were once beginners.

You could learn to tie flies without help from anyone. You could also invent or discover everything you need — techniques, tools, materials. Many already have. But that's the hard way; unless you're a bona fide genius that's not a very good way to learn anything. It's always easier to profit from the experience and ideas of those who came before.

That's the purpose of this book: to present in a progressive, readable, and highly graphic format all of the basic ideas and techniques you need to start tying flies. It is a primer addressed to the rank beginner, yet any serious student will complete this book able to tie virtually any fly. There are concepts, materials and even fly patterns which to my knowledge have never before appeared in print, contributions that I hope will make your introduction to the subject uniquely enjoyable.

You might say this book is the result of arrested development. Although I manage to tie flies well enough to deceive all the fish needed to keep me contented as a flyfisher and fly tier, I still feel as a tier pretty much a beginner. Many who learned to tie flies in the years since I first asked "What's a bobbin" have now reached a level of expertise that, for lack of time, dexterity and dedication I may never attain. Some of those individuals I'm proud to have had as students.

While I'm wont to marvel at the progress of other tiers, I've discovered that being "arrested" close to the threshold of ignorance is not really so bad. In fact, when it comes to the task of trying to write a book for beginners it is a decided asset. That and the ability to sketch a little. For one thing, it's much easier to identify with the student's introduction to the subject of tying flies and its often conflicting language, which at first seems like an illogical jargon intended to confuse rather than clarify. For another, it's not so difficult to recall one's own frustration with the awkward products of hand and eye. To offset those early embarrassments are the vivid memories of the immensely satisfied feeling I earned with my first properly tied fly, a pleasure exceeded only through the magic of a brown trout's frantic approval. I've also found it a great help to have many more questions than answers. In the search for simple explanations of ideas long accepted as fact, the biggest surprise has been not how much I know, but what I thought I knew. If for no other reason than to straighten and clarify my own thinking on the subject I needed to write this book. I invite you to read on in the sincere belief that "Fly Tying... Adventures in Fur, Feathers and Fun" will speak for itself.

John F. McKim

Acknowledgments

Sharing is half the fun. Fortunately, others feel as I do. In fact, the most outstanding, perhaps even unique, quality of most fly tiers is a willingness to share with others.

To identify all of the individuals and groups whose contributions to fly tying form the fabric of this book would be impossible. To be fair, the list would have to include not only everyone who ever gave his fly idea to another, but every student who asked a "stupid" question and every instructor who freely gave of his time and effort to explain the answer or show a way that something could be done. Yet, one of my reasons for writing this book is, in a sense, to repay through recognition those individuals who years ago opened their world to me and literally changed my life. Surely, the men of the Long Beach Casting Club, some of whom now live only in the hearts and minds of their friends, deserve a special thanks, for they were the ones who proved that even I could learn to tie flies. Indeed, the club's excellent Fly Tying "Menu," a compilation of more than forty years of the members' instruction, shared information and ideas was the inspirational basis for this book.

Among the individuals who deserve recognition are James R. Eriser, a past president of both the Long Beach Casting Club and the Federation of Fly Fishermen, who convinced me to succeed him as Editor of the FFF "Tie Flyer," and J. Stanley Lloyd, past Editor of the FFF Bulletin, of which the "Tie Flyer" was a part. The drawings and ideas herein are in large

measure an outgrowth of those four rewarding years with my friend Stan. I'm also indebted to others: John Hockenbrocht and Don Mollet, proprietors of the Hidden Rod Shop in Signal Hill, California who were always ready to offer constructive ideas and technical advice; Henry W. "Hank" Downs, my longtime fishin' podner and friend, who reviewed the book and approved; Evelyn Tomlinson and Norman Phillips, friends and fellow writers who encouraged me to write; Pat Brumm, my friend and magazine editor whose advice and approval gave me the confidence to continue; and James E. Handley, my book editor whose comments were both constructive and enthusiastic. The contribution of my wife, Joan, quite simply cannot be measured.

Factual data for the book was gleaned from a variety of sources, including knowledgeable and expert fly tiers, some of whose patterns are featured herein, manufacturers and fly materials dealers catalogs, and published works on the subject. Under "Sources" I have listed all available literature used as reference material, as well as other pertinent works.

As you enter the world of the fly tier you will find people of goodwill everywhere with a passion for hooks dressed in fur, feathers and fun. Remember, it is they who have already done most of the sharing. For the most part, this book has been my way of compiling and translating the best of their ideas for you.

John F. McKim

Contents

Featured Patterns

List of Figures and Plates

Tools & Materials

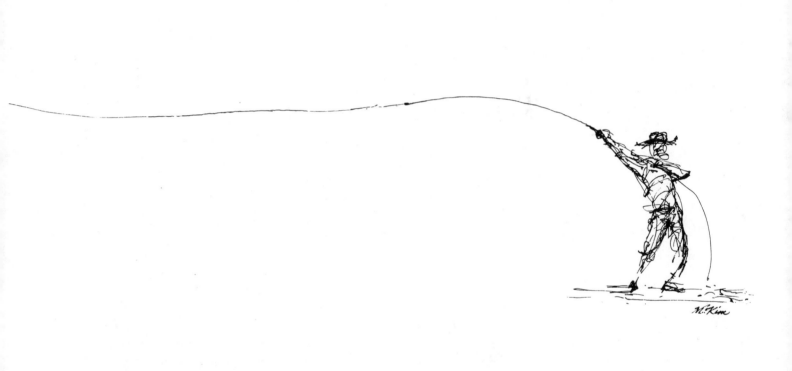

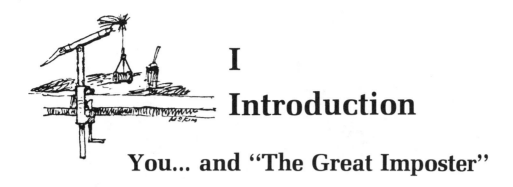

I
Introduction

You... and "The Great Imposter"

If you can tie a knot, you can tie a fly... NOW... before you read another word. Even if you've never tried to tie flies before, you can tie a fly that will catch a fish. Nearly everyone can. Tie a couple of small yellow or white feathers on a hook with a few wraps of sewing thread and a square knot and you'll have a dandy fly for bonito. A genuine fly that will really work. Tying flies can be just that simple.

Just what is a fly? In this book we mean a hook that has been disguised with various materials so as to attract and catch fish. Such artificial creations can be thought of as "The Great Imposters" of angling, for their sole purpose is to deceive. Some flies are expressly designed to simulate natural baits; others bear no specific resemblance to anything at all except themselves. Flies are tied in all sizes and shapes using a wide spectrum of natural and synthetic materials; there are thousands of patterns meant to take both fresh and salt water fish. The most important thing to remember is that the artificial fly *does* work, a fact that has been used to good advantage for thousands of years.

The fact that you've read this far should indicate that — at the very least — you're curious about the "art" of tying flies. Maybe you've always wanted to learn but never had the time or money. Or maybe this is the first time you've even been exposed to the idea. If you wish to learn, this book can help you. If you're determined to learn, you will.

It is a fact that very few individuals lack the native abilities to learn to tie simple flies. Sure, some will never be able to tie tiny, complex patterns, and we've seen people become totally discouraged by the mere sight of a beautifully crafted fly. Don't make that mistake. Remember, the person who tied the fly that seems so impossibly difficult for you started where you are now... at the beginning.

This book will not teach you to be a master fly tier. When you are finished with it you will still be more or less a beginner. If you wish to continue to learn, there is a wealth of published material on the subject — much of it directed toward the beginning and advanced student. In fact, the answers to virtually all questions you may have on fly tying — past and present — can be found in a book somewhere.

Nor will this book teach you to be a fly fisherman. Flyfishing is an entirely different, though related subject, not within the scope of this book.

For most people tying flies remains a hobby. Some find complete enjoyment in the tying itself and never fish at all. A few make it their career, although in terms of money it is seldom rewarding. If you're sure you will be tying flies for a long time, you will want the proper equipment to make the task easier. This book will show you the items you'll need, and I strongly recommend that you buy the very best equipment and materials you can afford. Fly tying equipment does not come cheap, but you will be using it for a long time and quality is always a good investment in terms of durability and function.

Maybe you'll be one of those — and there are many — who'll give fly tying a brief whirl, lose interest and go on to something new. I realize tying flies is not for everyone. If you're not really

sure and would rather not spend much to find out, I will show you that most of the items you'll need are already in and around your home and garage. You can easily make the basic tools and it can cost you little or nothing.

Everything in this book is designed to show you how to apply the common materials. I've made an honest and deliberate attempt to keep it simple, to make it easier for you to understand. Each succeeding fly pattern has been carefully selected to illustrate and introduce you to a different technique that will enable you to tie many other flies. When you have finished — and even before then — by all means go fishin'. Meanwhile, enter with me the world of fly tying...the land of "fur, feathers and fun."

What is fly tying?

A good question. From the name — fly tying — you might naturally assume that all flies are tied; that is, that all flies are always made by wrapping thread or threadlike material to bind other materials on a hook. Well, some flies are tied by bonding the materials to each other with adhesives. Others are tied by pinching the hook between folded metal. Are these flies really tied? In the strictest sense... no. But don't let that confuse you. Regardless of the methods used,

the process of fly construction is still referred to as tying the fly, or "dressing the hook."

How the hook is dressed is the only "secret" of fly tying. Of the several techniques used, relatively few are difficult to learn. With enough practice they'll become easy. Once you've learned how different materials can be tied to achieve specific effects you should be able to tie nearly any fly pattern you choose.

That's a term you might find confusing. Just what is a fly "pattern"? In a general sense, the pattern of any fly is the way its materials are put together to give it a distinct appearance. For instance: a general dry fly pattern can include an endless series of different flies, each tied to look almost exactly alike using similar but different materials and with no two flies the same color combination. Within that series you could also have a very specific pattern — say the "Quill Gordon" — in which the materials, the way they're tied, their relationships to each other, the colors and the proportions of the fly must appear identical in all sizes in which it's tied — or it cannot be called a "Quill Gordon." You can also tie another very specific pattern such as the "Woolly Worm" using identical types of materials, all tied precisely the same on the same sized hooks to look exactly alike in silhouette, and by just changing the colors have an endless series of different "Woolly Worms" — black, orange, white, variegated and so on. So you see, "the pattern" in fly tying can mean either a typical silhouette, a fly tied to very precise standards, or variations of a particular fly.

Pretty involved, huh? Well, that's lesson number one. The subject of fly tying can be as technically difficult and confusing as you choose to make it — or as simple. The hobby of fly tying can — and should always be — just plain fun. Relax, take it slowly one step at a time and concentrate on each new technique until you've mastered it completely.

Each of the so-called "patterns" in this book were carefully chosen to either introduce a new tying technique or help you to constructively polish one you've already learned. The ideal arrangement, of course, would also be one in which each succeeding tying technique and fly pattern are slightly more difficult to execute. That was my intent, and in a general sense things do become harder as you work through the book. However, should you find a pattern too difficult, skip to the following fly. You can always come back for a second try. No doubt, similar groups could be chosen from the many thousands of existing flies to illustrate the basic techniques. But learn to tie the flies in this book and you'll be able to tie nearly any fly you can see. With each succeeding fly your skills will improve. Skill is knowledge used effectively and your skill as a fly tier can only be developed through lots of practice. Tie at least six of each fly and you'll be ready to try the next one. Lest you think that all that time and effort will be wasted, don't worry. Each fly in this book was also selected because it has taken fish.

Of course, there'll be those times when everything goes wrong — when your fingers will seem like toes with dim-witted minds of their own. Times when you'll become impatient and discouraged. My advice? RELAX. Remember the words of the late Jim Quick: "It is much, much better to tie one fly in an hour's time... than a dozen that would be taken only by a trout with a sense of humor."

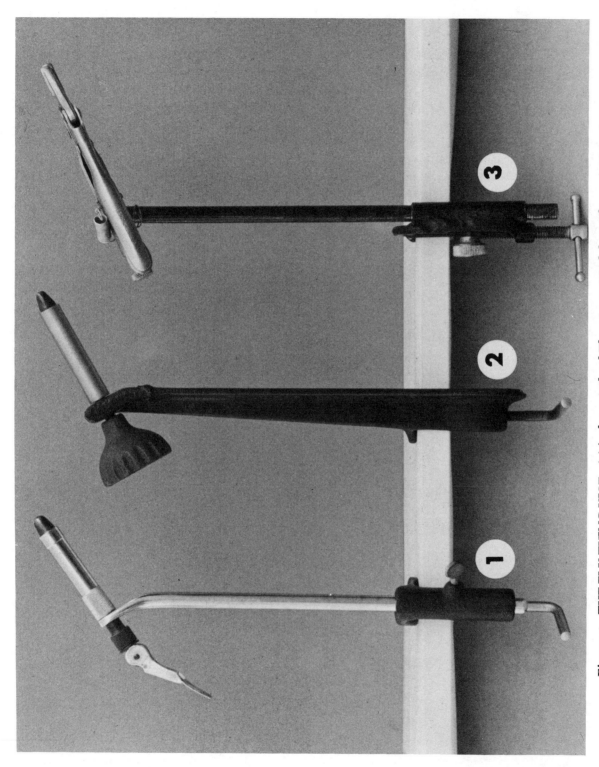

Figure 1. THE FLY TYING VISE. (1) is the standard Thompson Model "A" lever-action vise; (2) the standard Thompson Model "B" screw-knob action vise. Both are typical examples of the types of vises being marketed. (3) is a Lefty Kreh idea, a homemade vise that utilizes a small pair of Vise-Grip pliers to clamp and hold the hook.

II
Tools

Basic Fly Tying Tools

To tie flies you must have both materials and the tools to apply them. This includes all of the materials for each fly pattern in this book, an assortment of the types and sizes of hooks required, and a few basic fly tying tools. Everything you'll need can be purchased either at tackle stores that carry fly tying materials or through any of several fishing tackle catalog dealers. Some of the materials may also be found in yarn shops, department stores and other commercial outlets. You'll be surprised at what you can find just by snooping around.

If you intend to become a serious student of fly tying — especially if you plan to use your creations on fish — invest in the best set of tools you can afford. Quality is seldom cheap, and with today's inflationary trend, good tools will require a substantial cash outlay. But, properly maintained, quality fly tying tools will function indefinitely. They're a better long-term investment.

When it comes to materials, always tie your flies with the best quality you can find. It's false economy to tie with inferior materials. Consider the time and effort you'll have wasted if on the very first strike a weak hook breaks off in the fish's mouth — or the frustration and discouragement you will suffer trying to construct a quality dry fly using wet type materials, or tying a very small pattern with vastly oversized thread. It cannot be done. But you can and should practice the techniques of tying flies with substitutes whenever practicable. Considering the cost and increasing scarcity of high quality materials, that's just sensible economy.

When you get to the actual tying of the fly you'll soon discover that flies are tied as much by feel as with sight. In fact, to tie good flies you must learn to "see" with your fingers. It makes it a lot easier when you can see in clear detail what you're making, especially the colors of the different materials. But being color blind is not a significant handicap to many tiers and I have no doubt whatever that a totally non-sighted person with enough determination can learn to tie flies.

If you're a person blessed with good eyesight, protect it. Tying flies is close, meticulous work that without proper illumination — and for some, magnification — may result in severe eyestrain. Always tie in a well lit area with plenty of light directed upon the fly you're tying.

If you're lucky and have a place where you can set up shop permanently, make sure the table or bench is at a comfortable height and large enough to spread out your tools and materials. If not, you can either make a container to store all your fly tying items or buy one. Many tiers have found a plastic sewing box makes a fine portable kit in which to store fly tying tools and materials, almost as if it were designed for that purpose. You can probably find one in department stores or other outlets that stock sewing materials.

Now let's look at what you'll need to tie flies. Figure 1 and Figure 2 show typical examples of the basic tools. Everything you need, of course, can be purchased. A few of the items I've shown are, in fact, homemade substitutes. You should consider the vise, bobbin, bodkin, hackle pliers and scissors necessities, the rest optional.

Magnifiers. I have a strong (admittedly biased) suspicion that those who can't see

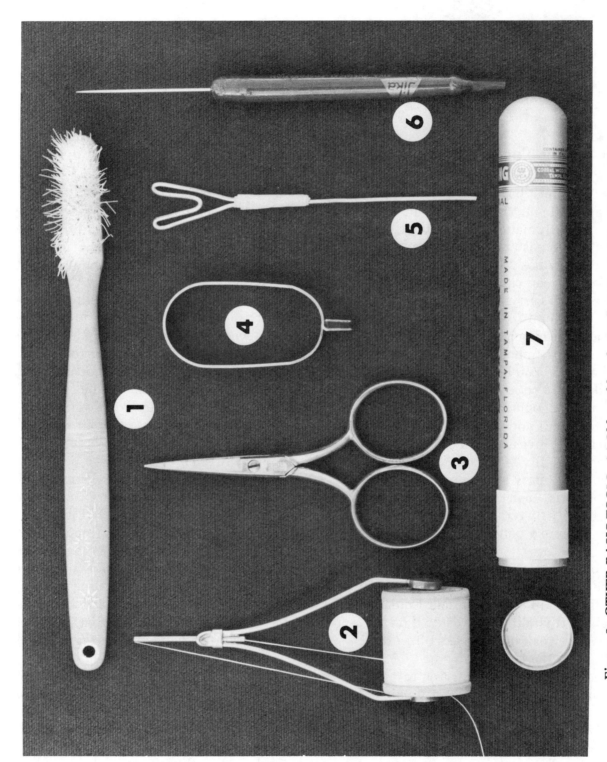

Figure 2. OTHER BASIC TOOLS. (1) Old toothbrush; (2) fly tying bobbin (Matarelli type shown with spool of thread in place); (3) small fly tying scissors; (4) standard hackle pliers of the type with one rubberized jaw; (5) homemade dubbing twister; (6) homemade bodkin, or dubbing needle; and (7) homemade hair tamper. All the basic tools are commercially available, of course. However, complete instructions for making homemade equivalents, including those shown here, are given in the Appendix.

anything good in fly tying just need glasses. In order to appreciate — or tie — a fly you must first be able to see it. If you're not sure even with glasses whether it's hackle or hair, better get a magnifier. They're available in all types from head visors to bench mounted magnifying lamps. Even a cheap pair of dimestore magnifying eyeglasses will do the job.

Fly Tying Vise. You must have something to hold the hook firmly while you're tying the fly. You could use your hand — a standard method in the long ago — but why do that when you can use a neat invention called a **fly tying vise.** You can always tie with your hands as a last resort — say along a stream — but a vise is easier.

There are many types and makes of vises available. All of them work on the same principle; that is, a pair of jaws open to accept the hook and close to squeeze it between them. Compression and friction hold the hook firmly in place. Jaw pressure is applied in some vises by screwing a knob or turning a handle, in others by forcing down a lever. Either type is fine. Two of the standard vises commonly used are shown in Figure 1.

One of the most important things about a vise is the size of its jaws. As a rule, the smaller the hook, the smaller the jaws should be. They should interfere as little as possible with your fingers while you're tying the fly. Small, narrow jaws can easily apply the pressures required to hold the smaller sized hooks, but as the hook size increases so does the force required to hold the hook. Sometimes, exerting the force needed to hold a large hook in a small-jawed vise causes the vise to become "jaw sprung." Then the vise is useless for tying very small flies.

If you can't afford two vises — one for small, the other for large hooks — recommend you select a standard vise that will accept the mid-range of hook sizes. Rest assured that all of the patterns in this book can be tied on a standard vise.

When choosing a vise, bear in mind that it should be sturdy and well-made, with forged and hardened steel jaws that have smooth contact surfaces. The jaws should be adjustable to accept the full range of common hooks and have a positive tightening system that will not allow the hook to work loose while you're tying the fly.

Price is not necessarily a measure of quality when it comes to fly tying vises. Some of the lower priced brands will outperform others costing twice as much. Currently, vises range from about $16.50 to more than $60.00. They may be purchased directly from fly tying shops or through any of several catalog dealers.

Let's just suppose you're a person who likes to tinker and would like to make your own vise. A surprisingly large number of people do. In that case, your product will be a direct reflection of your ingenuity, mechanical ability and the resources available to you. Sometimes a homemade tool is an improvement over commercial products made for the same purpose. Figure 1 also shows an excellent vise for mid-size to very large hooks that was constructed from the smallest model of Vise-Grip pliers. First, a ⅜-inch by 10-inch long steel rod (a diameter that fits the base clamp of many commercially manufactured vises) was brazed at a 45 degree angle to the screw adjusting handle. This suspends the pliers in the correct attitude for tying flies. Next, a short length of tubing just large enough inside to receive the rod was brazed to a common C-clamp and both clamp and tube were drilled and tapped for a threaded knob. The screw knob provides vertical support and adjustment. To prevent damage to the hook's finish, the jaws of the pliers were ground smooth. Incidentally, this idea of Lefty Kreh's is my favorite vise for tying large streamers, bucktails and jigs.

Actually, you don't have to be a welder to make a pliers vise. And the pliers don't have to

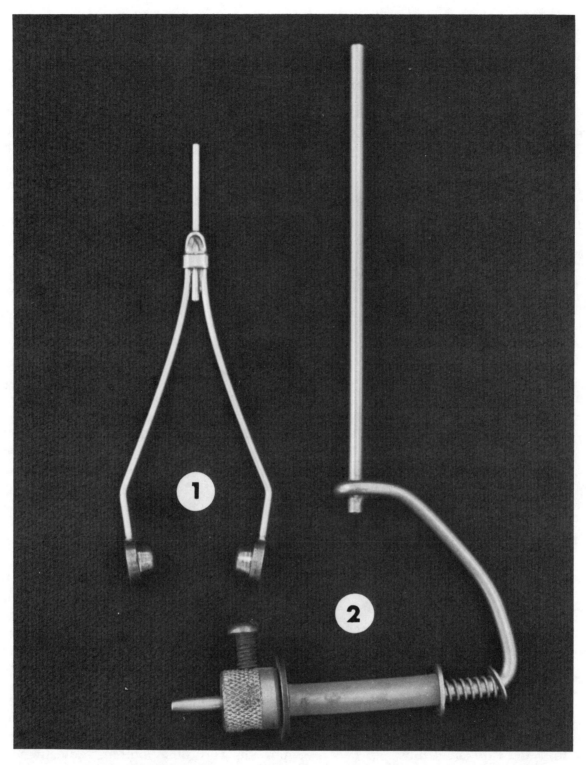

Figure 3. FLY TYING BOBBINS. Two examples of the types of bobbins being marketed are (1) the Matarelli and (2) the Buszek. There are others.

be the Vise-Grip type. A pair of common slip-joint pliers will do. The easy-to-build wooden stand shown in Appendix Plate 5 can easily be adapted to fit Vise-Grips, slip-joint or other types of pliers.

The biggest advantage to using Vise-Grips is that their unique pressure adjusting and locking design make it nearly impossible to spring the jaws, even with very large hooks. Common pliers lack this feature so an alternate method must be found to close and lock the jaws. To rigidly clamp a hook requires a surprising amount of pressure. (Test this yourself by squeezing the plier's handles while wiggling the hook.) We can provide the needed force in any one of several ways: by using hand pressure (a tiring and clumsy solution), compressing the handles in a bench vise, using a C-clamp to squeeze the handles or jaws, or by simply wrapping the handles with a series of stout rubber bands until the right pressure has been applied. There are probably others I've not thought of, but the method illustrated in Appendix Plate 5 does work. It's simple, effective and relatively easy to use. What's more, all of the materials you'll need are probably already in your home or garage.

Bobbin. To tie a fly requires a length of thread long enough to wrap all of the materials onto the hook and secure them in place. The thread must be under constant tension as well, otherwise it will become loose and ruin the fly. To perform this task in fly tying a tool called a **fly tying bobbin** is a great aid.

Of course, a bobbin is not absolutely necessary. Some tiers simply cut a length of thread, use their thumb and forefinger to regulate the tension while they're wrapping the fly and secure each stage as they finish with a half-hitch. If they want constant tension, it's easy to attach a clothespin or other weighted clamp to the thread and let it hang. But while that method works fine, a fly tying bobbin will do all

of that and more.

For one thing, a bobbin holds an entire spool of thread, so a continuous supply is always available. For another, it gives positive thread control, allowing you to tie the fly with just the right amount of tension on the thread. By squeezing the sides of the spool, the bobbin produces friction. If there's too little friction, the spool will turn and unwind the thread from just the weight of the spool and bobbin; too much may cause the thread to break. So, all bobbins are designed to regulate the pressure in order to smoothly release thread under the proper tension.

Good bobbins are also comfortable to hold in the hand. You'll find that the bobbins that feed thread through a small tube designed to be held between thumb and forefinger allow very precise control during the tying process.

Several styles of bobbins are offered for sale. In price they will range from about $4.00 to $6.00. The quality will vary with the manufacturer. Buy the style you are most comfortable using, but before you buy, make sure that the one you've chosen will accommodate the common sizes of thread spools and that it will be easy to switch spools. Make sure the spool turns smoothly and tension can be easily adjusted. Most importantly, check both edges of the feeder tube or hole through which the thread must pass. It must be free of burrs or grooves that can abrade, weaken and cause the thread to break. It's often a good idea to have several bobbins, each loaded with a different size or color of thread. Two common styles of fly tying bobbins are shown in Figure 3.

When you consider that a good bobbin almost never wears out, they're not prohibitively expensive, but if you prefer, Appendix Plate 6 illustrates how a serviceable bobbin can be made from items commonly found in the home.

Bodkin. Also called a **dubbing needle**. A bodkin is really just a handle with a long, sharp-pointed end. It's used to apply wax to the tying thread, to apply cement during the different stages of fly construction and to coat the head of the fly, to pick out guard hairs and hackle barbs that get tied down, to spread and arrange the barbs of spun hackle, and to pick the eye clean of dried cement. Some models feature a magnet or an open-eyed hook on the other end, the first to pick up small hooks, the second to hang the bodkin from when you're not using it.

Bodkins vary in price. A good one will cost about $3.00. If you can, try to keep several bodkins in your tying kit. One way to save money is to make your own. Appendix Plate 7 shows how to make a variety of homemade bodkins from items you may already have around your home. Or, you can simply stick a sewing needle in a small cork if you wish. There are many ways to make this essential tool.

Scissors. To tie flies you'll need at least one — preferably two — pairs of scissors. They're so indispensable many professional tiers just let them dangle from their finger while tying, ready for use. To be good for fly tying, they must be made from high quality forged steel with tight, smoothly operating parts and sharp cutting edges. The blades should taper to fine points that allow precise trimming of individual hackles and hairs. The finger holes should be oversized. Fly tying scissors with all these features are available in two sizes; an all-purpose standard model and an extra long model for maximum leverage in cutting larger bunches of hair and hackle. If you buy one pair only, buy the standard model. If you buy your scissors, by all means buy true fly tying scissors. They will cost no more than other scissors of comparable quality.

Of course, other types of scissors *can* be used to tie flies. As long as they're well made, any small straight-bladed scissors such as embroidery scissors will do. Just be sure you grind the points to needle sharpness.

Hackle Pliers. In tying flies it's often necessary to tightly wrap a feather repeatedly around the hook's shank and tie it down. Wrapped in the same spot, it's called a "spun" hackle; wrapped spirally along the shank it's a "palmer" hackle. With a decent sized feather it's easy to use your fingers. With small feathers the remaining tip is often too small to hold. To make the job less frustrating we use a small device called a **hackle pliers**. Squeeze the handles and the jaws open; release them and they close. That's the way most standard hackle pliers operate, and the best of those are the type with one rubberized jaw. They're less likely to cut or break the delicate tip of the feather. A pair of hackle pliers will cost up to about $3.00. See Figure 2.

Another device called the **E-Z Hook**, used in the electronics industry for pulling fine wire, and available in electronic supply stores, is rapidly gaining acceptance among fly tiers. Many prefer it to standard hackle pliers. In a pinch, just use any small clamping device that works for you.

Tooth Brush. Add an old tooth brush to your list of items. You'll find it's a great tool for brushing the soft underfur from deer body hair and bucktail. See Figure 2.

Hair Tamper. Sometimes you'll need to match up the tips of deer type hair or bucktail. Without some type of tool this is not an easy job. That's where a **hair tamper** comes in handy. Essentially, this is just a metal tube with a cap into which you slip a bunch of hairs butt end first. They must be brushed free of fuzz or they won't slide freely past each other. A few raps of the capped end on a hard surface is usually enough to align the tips so that when you remove the cap you're ready to tie.

Several brands of tamping tools are marketed. They run about $5.00. However, almost any capped metal tube will work. Appendix Plate 8 shows how to make one from a discarded aluminum cigar tube. Avoid plastic tubes; the static electricity generated causes the hairs to stick. To align properly, they need to slide past one another.

Tweezers. Another good tool to have. Fly tying tweezers come in several sizes and are very useful when you have to pick up small hooks, flies and other materials. A good pair should cost about a dollar.

Dubbed Loop Twister. One tying technique involves twisting a loop of sticky thread and fur together to form a kind of furry cord. You can buy a special dubbing twister for about $2.00; however, the homemade twister shown in Appendix Plate 8 does a dandy job.

Bobbin Threader. A very handy tool to add to your kit. After a period of use, you will find that wax from the tying thread has accumulated in the bobbin's thread feeder tube. While this will not detrimentally affect its operation to any great extent, such wax deposits make it hard to change thread or re-thread your bobbin in cases where the thread breaks. A bobbin cleaner is a simple dual purpose device consisting of a handle connected to a long narrow small diameter spring steel wire loop. It works like this: to clean the bobbin, push the loop through the feeder tube, pass a cotton cord through the end of the loop and withdraw the tool. The cord will drag the wax buildup along with it. To thread the bobbin, use the same procedure: insert the tying thread in the loop; withdraw the loop and thread and you're ready to tie. One brand of bobbin cleaner has a separate wire shaft to be used for cleaning. Bobbin cleaners are available for nominal cost from fly materials sources.

Half-hitch Tool. Later in Chapter 4 you will learn the uses of the half-hitch and one method of tying this useful knot without the need for a special tool. However, since there are some times when a half-hitching device comes in handy, you may wish to add one to your kit. Several types are available at nominal cost through fly materials sources.

Vise Material Clip. This is a small tempered steel clip that snaps onto the sleeve of any collet-type vise such as the Thompson "A" or "B" fly tying vises shown in Figure 1. Material clips are very useful for holding stray materials out of the way while other parts of the fly are being tied. The clip can be moved to any position. Material clips are available at nominal cost from fly materials sources.

Miscellaneous Items. These are not "musts," but to be really complete I'd like to recommend that you add a few more items to your kit. Believe me when I say, as your skills and interest grow you'll discover many other tools you'll want to have.

Keep a supply of facial tissues or paper towels handy. They'll come in mighty useful to clean up spills and wipe your tools clean. A hook hone or automotive point file is really a "must" to sharpen the larger hooks; most small sized high quality fly hooks are already sharp. A supply of round tooth picks will serve a jillion uses. So will a small cheap watercolor brush or two. Salvage an empty clear nail polish bottle; it makes an excellent head cement container with a built-in applicator brush for medium to large flies. Include a six inch plastic ruler to measure and check the proportions of your flies, and a pen or pencil and note pad to take notes.

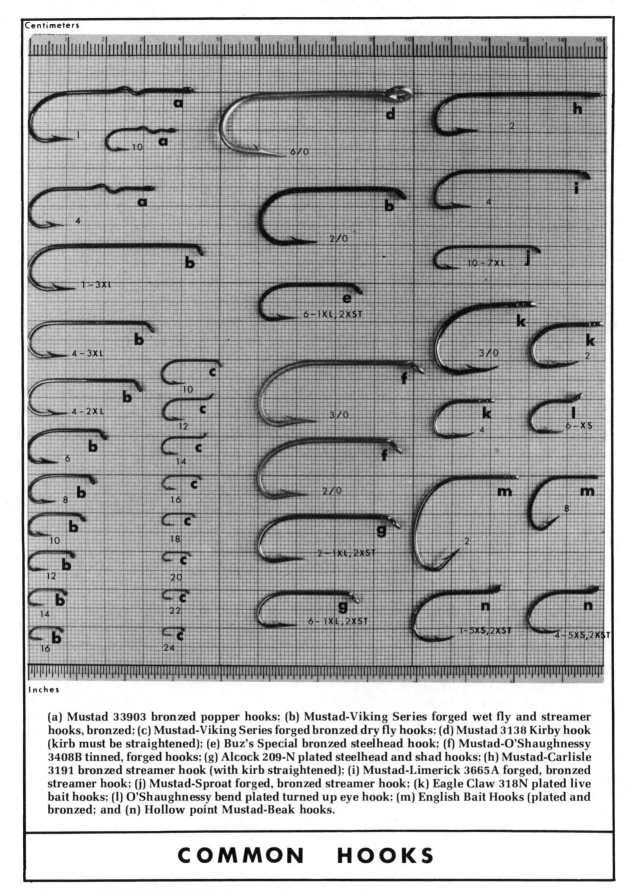

Centimeters

Inches

(a) Mustad 33903 bronzed popper hooks: (b) Mustad-Viking Series forged wet fly and streamer hooks, bronzed; (c) Mustad-Viking Series forged bronzed dry fly hooks: (d) Mustad 3138 Kirby hook (kirb must be straightened); (e) Buz's Special bronzed steelhead hook; (f) Mustad-O'Shaughnessy 3408B tinned, forged hooks; (g) Alcock 209-N plated steelhead and shad hooks; (h) Mustad-Carlisle 3191 bronzed streamer hook (with kirb straightened); (i) Mustad-Limerick 3665A forged, bronzed streamer hook; (j) Mustad-Sproat forged, bronzed streamer hook; (k) Eagle Claw 318N plated live bait hooks; (l) O'Shaughnessy bend plated turned up eye hook; (m) English Bait Hooks (plated and bronzed; and (n) Hollow point Mustad-Beak hooks.

COMMON HOOKS

Figure 4. COMMON HOOKS. Some of the patterns and sizes of hooks used to tie flies. Hooks similar to those shown are usually offered by other hook makers.

III
Materials

As you can see, the tools of fly tying *can* cost you little or nothing, just the time and effort to construct. But what about materials? Don't you need real fly tying materials to construct flies? The answer to that is yes... and no. What I mean is, if you simply want to learn the techniques — the process — of tying flies, you needn't buy a thing. You can easily substitute.

For example, it is no more difficult to tie a fly on a needle, a nail or a safety pin than on a hook. And it's a whole lot cheaper. Quality fly hooks are expensive and becoming more so all the time. Tying thread? Still no problem; common sewing thread is at least adequate to demonstrate the tying techniques. In fact, plain sewing thread can be an acceptable first choice for some large saltwater patterns. The home sewing kit is often an excellent source for yarn, floss and similar natural and synthetic materials. Indeed, a great many fly tying materials were originally developed for the seamstress.

But what about feathers and fur? Aren't most fishing flies made from one or both? Yes. From earliest times the various kinds of fur, hair and feathers have always been the mainstays of the fly tier's craft. But that poses no problem for you either. There's usually a family pet who won't miss a little fur (or feathers), a hunter friend who'll lend a hand, a feather-stuffed pillow or outmoded hat — and the forgotten treasures of the basement or attic. In fact, these are often sources of first-rate materials. Even clear nail polish will do for head cement.

All right, I've talked about substitutes, but if you're like most beginners, you want a product, not an exercise, a product that will impress Mr.

Trout or Mrs. Bass, not just a novelty to show your friends.

Right now you're probably wondering: "Okay, but when can I get started tying flies?" My answer is: if you really feel you must, then you can get started whenever you like. To learn the various techniques in Chapter 4 all you need are a few basic tools, a spool of thread and less than a dozen other kinds of materials. You can always refer back to the balance of this chapter and to the "Glossary of Fly Tying Materials" for answers to your questions on specific materials; you'll need to do so from time to time anyway.

But I strongly urge you to resist the temptation. I firmly believe it would be a mistake for you to skip the discussion of materials that follows. Take each step of this book in its normal progression. Read (and re-read if necessary) this and the preceding chapter on tools. A clear understanding of the functions of the basic tools and the differences in materials will help you learn the techniques — and ultimately tie the fly — a lot easier.

Now, let me anticipate your next question: "What kinds of materials will I need to tie quality flies?" Or put in another way: "What are the differences between the various materials that determine a fly's quality?" In the rest of this chapter I've tried to shed some light on that subject. There are so many different materials used to tie flies that to adequately describe them all, and the ways they are used, would be a book in itself. As a matter of fact, a number of fine books devoted to the subject of fly tying materials and techniques already exist, a few of which are listed in the section titled "Sources."

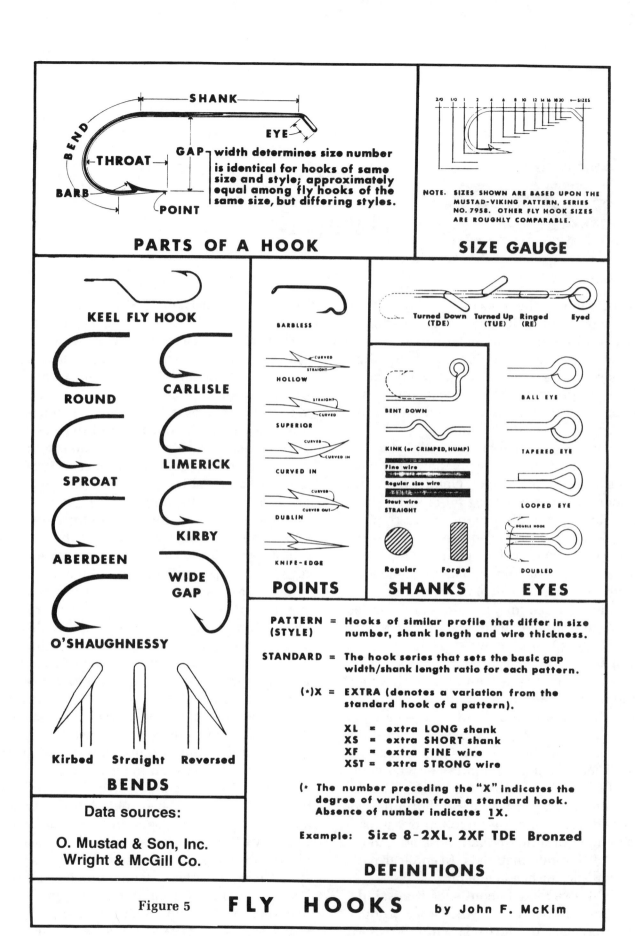

PARTS OF A HOOK

SHANK

BEND

EYE

THROAT

GAP — width determines size number is identical for hooks of same size and style; approximately equal among fly hooks of the same size, but differing styles.

BARB

POINT

SIZE GAUGE

2/0 1/0 1 2 4 6 8 10 12 14 16 18 20 ← SIZES

NOTE. SIZES SHOWN ARE BASED UPON THE MUSTAD-VIKING PATTERN, SERIES NO. 7958. OTHER FLY HOOK SIZES ARE ROUGHLY COMPARABLE.

KEEL FLY HOOK

ROUND

CARLISLE

SPROAT

LIMERICK

ABERDEEN

KIRBY

WIDE GAP

O'SHAUGHNESSY

Kirbed   Straight   Reversed

BENDS

POINTS

BARBLESS

HOLLOW — CURVED, STRAIGHT

SUPERIOR — STRAIGHT, CURVED

CURVED IN — CURVED, CURVED IN

DUBLIN — CURVED, CURVED OUT

KNIFE-EDGE

SHANKS

BENT DOWN

KINK (or CRIMPED, HUMP)

Fine wire

Regular size wire

Stout wire

STRAIGHT

Regular   Forged

EYES

Turned Down (TDE)   Turned Up (TUE)   Ringed (RE)   Eyed

BALL EYE

TAPERED EYE

LOOPED EYE

DOUBLE HOOK

DOUBLED

DEFINITIONS

PATTERN (STYLE) = Hooks of similar profile that differ in size number, shank length and wire thickness.

STANDARD = The hook series that sets the basic gap width/shank length ratio for each pattern.

(·)X = EXTRA (denotes a variation from the standard hook of a pattern).

XL = extra LONG shank
XS = extra SHORT shank
XF = extra FINE wire
XST = extra STRONG wire

(· The number preceding the "X" indicates the degree of variation from a standard hook. Absence of number indicates 1X.

Example: Size 8-2XL, 2XF TDE Bronzed

Data sources:

O. Mustad & Son, Inc.
Wright & McGill Co.

Figure 5   **FLY HOOKS**   by John F. McKim

You may wish to check into them later. As a beginner, though, it is important only that you gain a clear understanding of the basic categories of materials, such as:

Hooks
Binding and Bonding Materials
Fur and Hair
Feathers
Other Non-metallic Fiber Materials
Metal and Metalized Materials
Elastomeric and Buoyant Materials

Hooks.

Here's where quality really counts... right in the fish's mouth. But to list all the hooks upon which you could tie flies is far beyond the scope of this book. One manufacturer alone — O. Mustad & Son — makes over 30,000 different types and Mustad is just one of many hook makers! Figure 4 shows some of the common types and sizes of hooks used to tie flies.

Luckily, most manufacturers offer a series of different types, or **patterns** (there's that word again) that are made especially for tying flies. Each hook pattern is produced in a range of numbered sizes. The relative sizes within the series are determined by the width of the **gap** of the hook. The gap and other parts are shown in Figure 5. Unfortunately, the size numbers of different patterns never exactly correspond to one another. A Size #10 hook of one pattern may be somewhat larger or smaller than the Size #10 hook of a different pattern — even among differing patterns made by the same manufacturer. To determine the actual dimensions of a particular hook one must know its size, pattern (or style) number and whose product it is. This is simplified to some degree by the fact that there are relatively few patterns of fly hooks. Though hook proportions and designs differ widely, the size numbers of fly hooks do provide a general guide to the size of the hook. In other words, the width of the "gap" of a given size hook is very similar throughout most patterns of fly hooks.

All right, how do you select the right hook? The answer is dependent upon the functions expected of a hook in different situations. You should above all expect the hook to be sharp enough to hook the fish and strong enough to take the pressure without breaking. That is, it must be forged or tempered to hold a point and be as strong as possible for its size. It must resist straightening, yet not be so brittle as to easily break. Unless you're an expert, your best bet is to rely on the standard products of well-known hook makers. That's no guarantee, but I feel it's sound advice.

Next, a hook must suit the type of fly being tied. To float well, a dry fly requires a hook made from lightweight fine wire, while heavier wire stock is an asset in a sinking fly. The overall shape and size of the hook is also important. It must suit the silhouette and proportions desired in the finished fly.

The hook's finish is another factor. A smooth finish makes it easier to spin deer hair around the shank. Certain finishes and alloys, such as stainless steel, also help to resist corrosion, though this is not always a desirable quality; in fact, a saltwater pattern is best tied on a tinned, forged hook. Lost in a fish it will corrode away in a few days to leave the fish unharmed and ready for the next angler who happens along.

So, except for the sizes and types specified for each of the fly patterns in this book, the choice of hook is strictly your own. If you're a serious angler you'll choose the best.

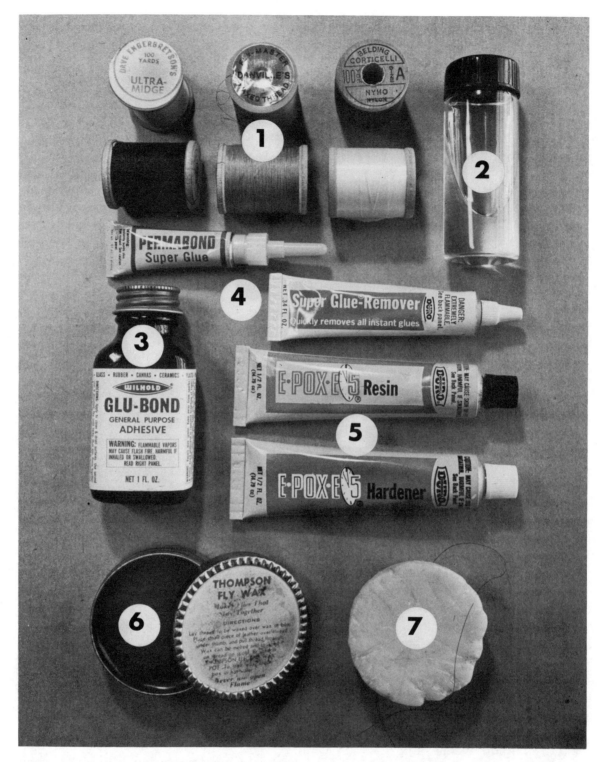

Figure 6. BINDING AND BONDING MATERIALS. Examples of the types of materials used to construct and secure the parts of a fly are: (1) tying threads, (2) head cement, (3) high strength rubber-type adhesive, (4) instant (cyanoacrylate) glue and instant glue remover, (5) 5-minute clear 2-part epoxy, (6) soft dubbing wax, and (7) hard tying thread wax.

16

Binding and
Bonding Materials

The types of materials used to wrap other parts of the fly on the hook and bind and bond them securely in place are shown in Figure 6.

Tying Thread. Fly tying threads are special products made from nylon or silk fibers, each designed to provide maximum strength for its size. Most modern threads are made of nylon, available in the form of multi-filament flat or twisted strands, and flat or round mono-filaments. Some threads are pre-waxed for strength; others are not. In size, they range upward from the smallest — No. 18/0 one-ply mono and No. 8/0 stranded — to Size A, the best size for beginning fly tiers. Sizes 8/0 to 6/0 are preferred for small to medium fly patterns; sizes 3/0 to A for most others. Until you develop skill with the bobbin, you may have difficulty with the small sizes. Most but not all tying threads are offered in black, white and a selection of colors.

Few sewing threads are suitable for fly tying. With the exception of Nymo, an excellent flat stranded thread, they're either too bulky, too weak or are made of fibers with inferior fly tying properties. Unfortunately, you probably will not be able to obtain Nymo. It's no longer made and existing supplies are fast running out. However, another flat stranded thread, Mono-Cord, for all intents and purposes is identical to Nymo. It's available in a good selection of colors, both waxed and unwaxed, in sizes 3/0 and A.

Adhesives. To make your fly durable you must use some type of glue or sticky substance during its construction, or at least to coat the head when you've tied off the thread, otherwise it's sure to come apart sooner or later. No single adhesive is perfect for every purpose. Each has its good as well as bad points.

The most commonly used adhesive is **head cement**, so-called because it's designed to provide a smooth durable coating on the head of the finished fly. In practice, head cements are used throughout the fly's construction; however, when tying a dry fly it's wise to thin the cement and apply it sparingly or the fly may become too heavy to float properly.

Most head cements are lacquer or acrylic-based liquids, each with its own specific thinner. Always use the correct thinner to keep your head cement thinned to the proper consistency; that is, thinned enough to flow smoothly into the fly's parts but not so thin as to soak all surfaces, making them stiff. If you leave the cap off the bottle for any length of time you'll have to thin your head cement. It has a tendency to thicken when exposed to the air. Although colored lacquers are also available, standard head cements are made as clear, colorless products so as to affect the natural colors of fly materials as little as possible. Acrylics and lacquers are well suited to fresh water use but are subject to deterioration in salt water.

For flies where you don't mind a slight color change, a high strength rubber type adhesive such as "Glu-Bond" by Wilhold, or "Pliobond" by Goodyear, makes an excellent all purpose bonder for both fresh and saltwater patterns. This type of adhesive can be thinned with MEK (Methyl Ethyl Ketone) solvent or acetone.

For saltwater flies and other large-headed sinking patterns the two-part epoxy glues are just great...nearly indestructible. Usually, the slow-setting types are best to use during the tying of the fly. The 5-minute type makes an excellent head coating and can also be applied whenever its fast-setting property is not detrimental to the tying operation. Make sure the epoxy you choose is the clear type.

Vinyl cement, Ambroid Model Cement and other special purpose adhesives have proved useful for certain fly tying applications. However, in my experience the so-called "super glues" (cyanoacrylates) cannot be relied upon to

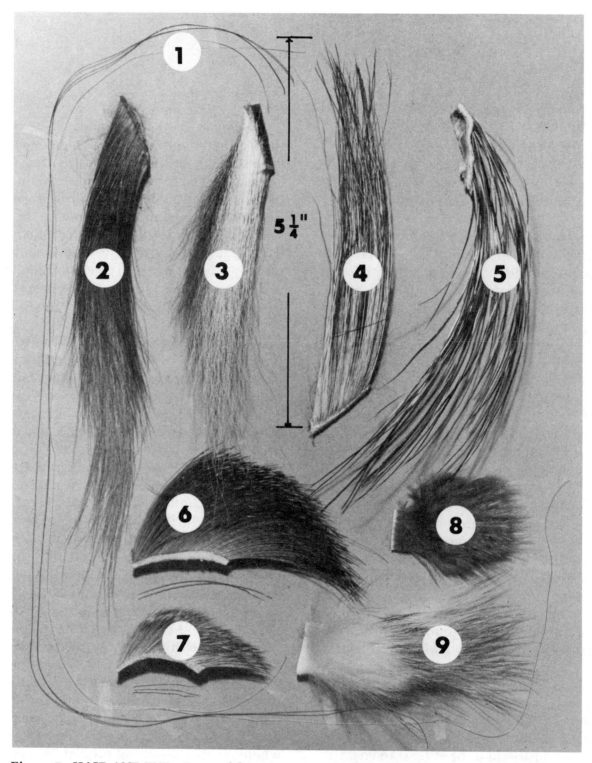

Figure 7. HAIR AND FUR. Some of the many types of hairs and underfur used to tie flies: (1) black and white horse hair; (2) dyed bucktail; (3) natural bucktail; (4) moose mane; (5) javalina; (6) and (7) large and small deer body hair; (8) muskrat; and (9) rabbit furs.

always bond properly and are dangerous to handle. Use them with extreme caution; they can cause blindness. Keep a tube of "super glue remover handy to un-stick fingers and remove unwanted glue from parts.

Waxes. Wax serves two very important functions in fly tying, each requiring a special type of wax. Grade No. 1 is a hard beeswax type wax used to coat tying threads to make them stronger and smoother to tie with. Grades No. 2 and 3 are soft, sticky waxes used to "dub" fur. This is the technique where the thread is coated with sticky wax (or another sticky substance), loose fur is applied and the two are twisted together to form a sort of furry strand. So-called **dubbing wax** comes in Grade No. 2, a tacky grade for dubbing or general work and Grade No. 3, a very tacky grade for controlling stiff or wiry furs. All three grades serve another important function: to help to bind the other fly materials together. To do this they must be specially formulated compounds that will not melt and run during warm weather, the main reason that common paste waxes and parafin are unsuitable for tying flies.

Many tying threads come prewaxed, others do not, so it's wise to have some Grade No. 1 handy. You'll also want to obtain a can of Grade No. 3 for dubbing.

Fur and Hair

Fur is a term commonly used to describe the soft hairy growth that covers nearly all parts of the bodies of some mammals. Its function is to protect and insulate the skin. Actually, what is called "fur" is a mixture of two types of hairs whose individual characteristics vary widely among different families of animals.

Protection is afforded by the **guard hairs**, long lustrous and usually straight fibers that shed water easily. Some animals such as man produce only this type of hair. On so-called fur bearing animals another type of hair called **underfur** lies below the guard hairs. Underfur is a dense layer of soft silky hairs one-half to three-quarters the length of the guard hairs that acts to create air pockets which help to warm and maintain body temperature. Some mammals have no underfur, while the coats of others are mostly hairs of this type.

Although some hairs are much longer and thicker than other types, this doesn't necessarily mean they're stronger. As a rule, the strength of a hair fiber increases with its density. In relation to their diameters the dense, shiny hairs of man, horse and cow are actually much stronger than the thick deer-type hairs. Members of the deer family — deer, moose, elk, caribou and the like — produce a very special hair that has an air-filled easily compressed cellular structure. In fact, its compressibility gave rise to the popular though erroneous notion that deer hair is "hollow." Though not a truly hollow fiber, deer body hair is extremely buoyant, a fact that's used to advantage in popping bass bugs and other flies where flotation is desired. The longest hairs of this type — bucktail and moose mane — are used in streamer fly applications where length, not strength, is important.

Sometimes strength *plus* length is required. For example, the hair itself may be used as a tying thread. This is where the dense, uniformly thick mane and tail hairs of members of the horse family — horses, mules and the like — can be put to good use. Horse hair is probably the only common animal hair that's long and strong enough to weave the complex, extremely durable bodies of woven-bodied flies.

The sheer diversity of hair types is a valuable asset to the fly tier. Techniques have been developed that take advantage of these physical differences. Tied singly, or in combination with other types, almost any aesthetic or functional result can be attained. Also, most hairs can be bleached and dyed to a desired color or shade, so that an infinite variety of hue and tone can be achieved by mixing dyed and/or natural underfurs in a kitchen blender.

To tie with underfur, or a mixture of underfur and guard hairs, involves the process called **dubbing** mentioned earlier. To dub fur, you simply apply the fur sparsely to a tying thread coated with a sticky substance and twist the two together to form a sort of furry strand. The strand (also called "dubbing," which often confuses the beginner) is then used to wrap the bodies of some types of flies.

Typical of the many types obtainable from fly materials dealers and elsewhere are the different furs and hairs shown in Figure 7. Others, including polar bear hair and seal fur, can no longer be bought or sold. These are but two of the totally protected animals which have been placed on the Rare and Endangered Species List. Attempts to reproduce the outstanding qualities of polar bear and seal using synthetic fibers have so far met with varying degrees of success. Some are not very good imitations. Others do a commendable job; indeed, it can be said in fairness that several substitutes offered may be the fiber of choice for certain flies.

Feathers

This is one natural product the fly tier would be hard put to do without. In the feather, nature has provided both bird and fly tier with a near perfect material for his purpose. Feathers come in many types, shapes, colors, shades, patterns and decorative and functional designs, and are easily dyed to create still others, so that when combined and tied in different ways it's possible to achieve almost any effect you wish.

Feathers are the unique clothing of birds. Each feather is in fact a renewable machine that is a true marvel of efficiency. Some feathers are designed to lift, propel, support and control flight. Others regulate the bird's body heat loss in both cold and hot climes, help to keep the bird dry, and in water birds provide flotation (an oily secretion acts as a water repellent). The decorative plumage of some birds seem to be designed to deceive enemies, attract a mate, or

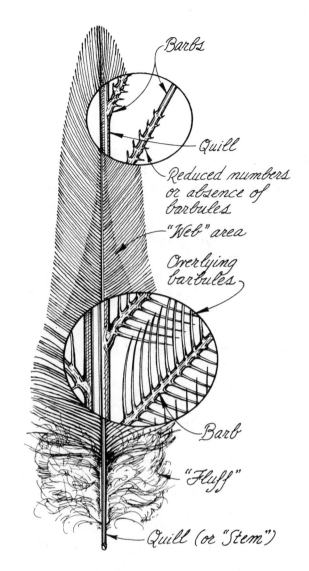

Figure 8. STRUCTURE OF A FEATHER. In the type of feather shown (hackle), barbicels are lacking; thus, the barbs are relatively free to move with respect to each other.

both. In fly tying, only the mature flight, contour and decorative plumage feathers are normally used.

Amazingly, all feathers of all birds are basically alike; subtle changes in the sizes, shapes and numbers of its component parts tailor each feather to a specific task. A typical feather consists of a central shaft called the **quill** (or **stem**) from each side of which branch fibers called **barbs** that grow outward and upward parallel to one another as they leave the quill. Barbs, in turn, have small branches along each side called **barbules,** collectively referred to in fly tying as the "web." The size and frequency of the barbules have much to do with how the feather acts: if the barbs are closely spaced and

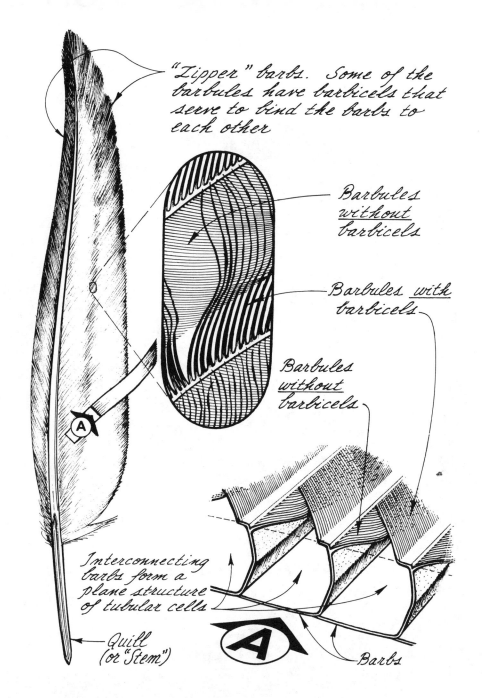

"Zipper" barbs. Some of the barbules have barbicels that serve to bind the barbs to each other

Barbules without barbicels

Barbules with barbicels

Barbules without barbicels

Interconnecting barbs form a plane structure of tubular cells

Quill (or "Stem")

Ⓐ

Barbs

Figure 9. THE TYPICAL FLIGHT FEATHER. In this type of feather, barbicels, tiny hook-shaped projections on the barbules, serve as nature's "zipper" to produce the smooth vane-like surface needed for flight.

have pronounced barbules, the barbules of one barb overlie the barbules on adjacent barbs and tend to hold the barbs together by friction, producing a "webby" effect. Barbules that don't overlie each other allow the barbs to move relatively free of one another. Figure 8 is an example of this type of feather.

Some, but not all, types of barbules bear **barbicels,** numerous tiny projections, many of which are hook-shaped at their tip. When present, barbicels function as a sort of natural "zipper," interlocking with the surfaces of adjacent barbules to mechanically bind the barbs all together. This produces a feather with a smooth vane-like surface, such as the typical flight feather illustrated in Figure 9. If pried apart, the barbs are easily reattached and the surface repaired like new by stroking between thumb and finger. As we'll see, barbules and barbicels determine to a great extent the ways we are able to use feathers to tie flies.

Hackle. Hackles are the types of feathers that

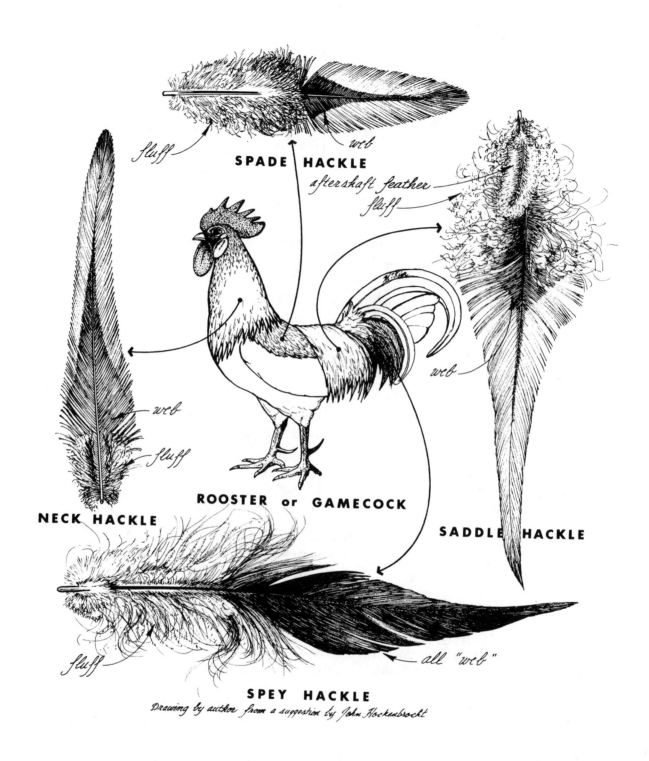

fluff

web

SPADE HACKLE

aftershaft feather

fluff

web

NECK HACKLE

web

fluff

ROOSTER or GAMECOCK

SADDLE HACKLE

fluff

all "web"

SPEY HACKLE
Drawing by author from a suggestion by John Hockenbrockt

Figure 10. HACKLE FEATHERS. The four types of hackle feathers found on the rooster — male — chicken and gamecock. Hen hackles are all web.

grow on the bird's neck and along its upper back to the tail. As a rule, when we refer to hackle we mean the types of hackle feathers produced by the various species and breeds of wild and domesticated chickens, all of whom are probably related to the present day wild jungle fowl of southeast Asia. However, the hackle feathers of other game birds are also used. One example, the hackle feather of the golden pheasant — called a **tippet** — is used to construct the famous "Royal Coachman" dry fly. In this case, barbs are stripped from the quill and used for the tail.

The hackle feathers most used by fly tiers are plucked from the male bird, or rooster chicken. There are four distinct types. See Figure 10. The **neck** hackles are narrow, relatively stiff-quilled feathers that solidly cover the neck and back of the head. **Spade** (or shoulder) hackles are short, wide hackles found on the bird's back and on the shoulders of his wings. **Saddle** hackles are long, slim feathers with long barbs and flexible quills that grow between the spade hackles and the tail. Finally, the **spey** hackles are the feathers on the sides of the tail near its base. Each type is used for different purposes.

All hackles are characterized by closely spaced barbs with barbules varying in both size and number. There are no barbicels, thus the barbs are relatively free to move with respect to one another. Most rooster hackles contain some "web," easily identified as the rather distinct triangular area on both sides of the central quill, widest near the butt and tapering toward the tip. Outside the triangular webbed area the barbs appear as individual fibers, stiff and polished looking. Unlike the rooster, the hen's hackle feather is all web. The extent of the web area is one measure of the feather's possible use. Because "webby" hackles absorb water readily, they should not be used as spun-type hackles on dry flies.

Actually, when I speak of a hackle as being **dry**, or as being **dry fly quality**, I'm really describing a feather with little or no web and

stiff, polished barbs bearing minute barbules or none at all. By contrast, the barbs of **wet** hackle are soft and "feathery." A simple test to distinguish between the two is to hold the tip of the feather with one hand while you gently stroke the barbs toward the butt of the quill with the other. If the barbs stand stiffly out from the quill at about a 45 degree angle and parallel to each other, the hackle is "dry." If, on the other hand, the barbs all cling together in clusters the hackle is "wet" (Figure 11). Another measure of "dry" quality for spun hackles are the proportions of the feather itself. The shorter the barbs with respect to the total feather length, the better the quality. Conversely, the long stiff polished barbs of spade hackles make excellent tails for dry flies. Saddle and spey hackles can also be used for the parts of dry flies, but they're usually best employed in streamer flies where

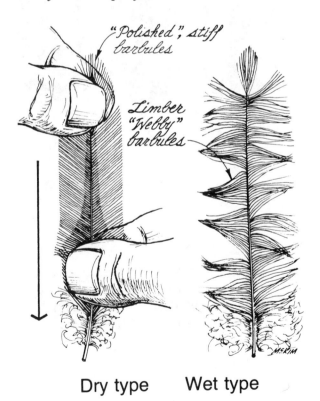

Dry type   Wet type

Figure 11. It's easy to determine whether a hackle is "dry" or "wet". Just stroke the barbs down toward the butt of the quill.

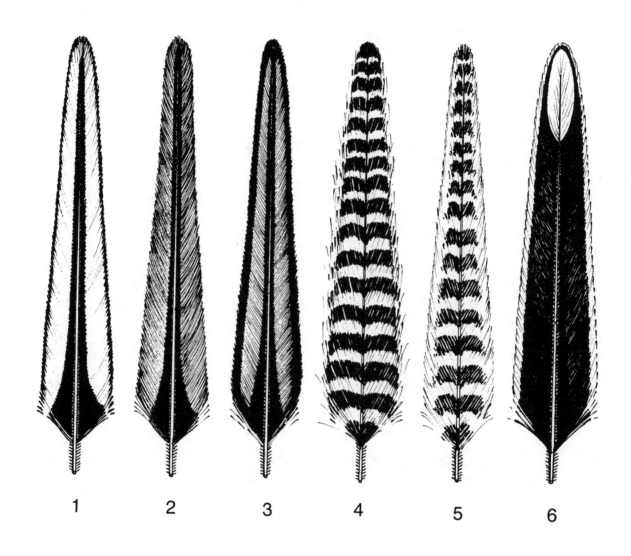

Figure 12. NATURAL HACKLE MARKINGS. Typical examples of the distinctive light/dark patterns of various hackles. Colors vary widely within each type. Common names for each include: (1)Badger; (2) Furnace; (3) Cock-y-bondhu; (4) Grizzly (black and white or a Variant such as Cree (color); (5) Monkey; and (6) Narobi.

their limberness and greater lengths are an asset.

Today, the best fly tying hackle comes from gamecocks raised abroad and imported into this country, and from some breeds of domestic birds that have been scientifically raised on special hormonal diets. To be of suitable quality, the birds must have molted at least two times. With one notable exception — the commercially bred and reared so-called "Super Grizzlies" — only wild or range-reared birds produce hackles of high dry fly quality.

It is clear that to correctly describe a hackle you must know whether it's from a hen or rooster, the area from which it was plucked and its physical characteristics. Thus, a typical description might be: **rooster neck** hackle of **medium dry** quality. If this were all, selection would be relatively easy. But, as if to confuse the beginner, hackles are often referred to as **grizzly** hackles, **badger** hackles and so on. This stems from the fact that certain names have been given to feathers on the basis of distinctive colors and light and dark patterns. The light/dark variations along each barb combine to create decorative markings recognizable through a wide range of colors and tones. Some of the common markings and the names by which they are identified are shown in Figure 12. These markings and the various natural colors associated with them are the results of cross-breeding between the different kinds of poultry.

While color plays an important role in the tied fly, of at least equal significance are its light/dark markings. These directly govern the finished look of a fly's spun hackle. Let's see if I can make that a little clearer: say we spin two hackles, one of "badger," one of "furnace." Both feathers have similar markings — a dark web area fading to lighter barbs — but the badger hackle's barbs are all dark tipped. Thus, when spun both will appear darkish near the hook, lighter toward the tips of the barbs. However, the badger hackle appears to have a darkish halo as well. Other effects can, of course, be obtained by using differently marked hackles or combinations of hackles.

Hackles can be purchased in two ways: as loose feathers or attached to the bird's skin. The very best neck hackles are sold as so-called intact **necks**, (also known as **capes**). You can buy saddle hackles still attached to the skin or strung together by a thread sewn through the butt of the quill. High quality feathers are available both ways. Necks and saddles as well as other loose feathers are packaged as both **natural** (the natural color of the bird) or **dyed** feathers, some dyed radiantly with fluorescent dyes that give extreme brilliance to their respective colors.

Primaries and Secondaries. The large feathers located along the trailing edges and tips of a bird's wing and used for flight are called **primary** and **secondary** feathers. The **primaries** (also called **pointers**) are the first six long, pointed feathers on the wing's tip. **Secondaries** (also called **flight** feathers) are the ten shorter, blunter feathers nearer the bird's body. All flying birds have feathers of this type, but only the primaries and secondaries of waterfowl such as ducks and geese are normally used to tie flies. (Figure 13)

Except for an area of webby fluff near the butt of the quill, all of the barbs of primaries and secondaries are "zipped" together; that is, tightly connected to one another by barbicels. This results in a vane-like surface that's ideal for many fly tying applications. For example, sections of barbs trimmed off near the quill are used to form the wings of dry fly and streamer patterns, the wingcases of nymphs large and small, and the tails of various flies. Paired wings are made from matched sections of barbs trimmed from left and right wing feathers that closely match each other in shape and size. Similarly, individual barbs trimmed from the leading edges of right and left goose primary feathers are used as the tails of certain nymph patterns.

Contour Feathers. The feathers that cover and shape the bird's body are **contour** feathers. Hackle forms the neck and back; **breast** and

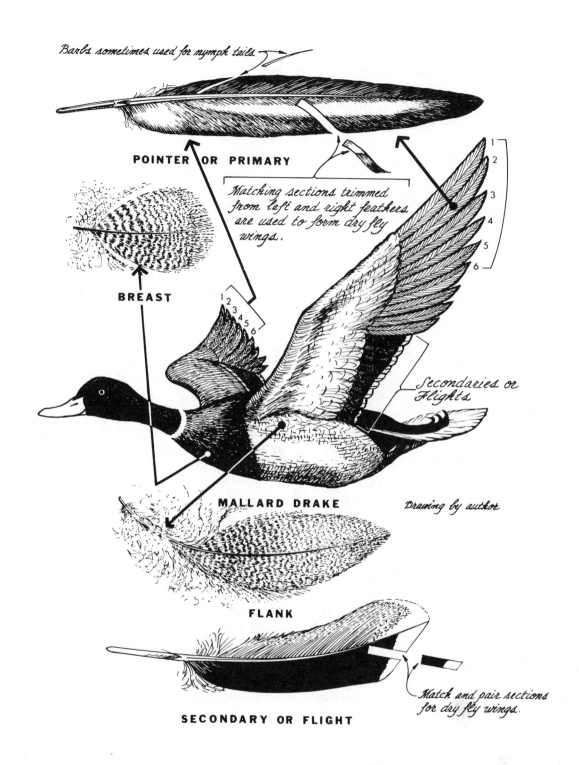

Barbs sometimes used for nymph tails

POINTER OR PRIMARY

Matching sections trimmed from left and right feathers are used to form dry fly wings.

BREAST

Secondaries or Flights

MALLARD DRAKE

Drawing by author

FLANK

Match and pair sections for dry fly wings.

SECONDARY OR FLIGHT

Figure 13. WATERFOWL FEATHERS. The four types of waterfowl (ducks and geese) feathers commonly used to tie flies, and some of the ways different parts are used. Of course, various other feathers from these birds are also employed for certain patterns.

flank feathers form the breast and sides. On the chicken only hackle is used; other contour feathers are taken from waterfowl and other gamebirds — ducks, geese, pheasants, grouse, partridge, guinea fowl and so on. Typically, such contour feathers on waterfowl are as follows:

Breast Feathers covering the breast and lower throat are short, wide, curved, stiff-quilled and have barred markings. They are fully barbuled and webby, making them water absorbant, best used for wet flies.

Flank Feathers are wide, oblong pointed feathers with distinctive markings. The barbs are long, closely spaced, soft, limber and heavily webbed throughout their lengths. They readily absorb water. We use both the complete feather and clumps of barbs stripped from the quill to tie various wet fly, nymph and streamer patterns.

Breast type feathers can be used to construct dry fly wings and bodies as long as the fly is treated afterward with a water repellent liquid or spray. The "Two-Feather Mayfly" is a fine example.

Contour feathers are designated by the type of bird and the area from which they were plucked. For example: Mallard flank or breast (shown in Figure 13), Teal breast, etc. They're sold in packages of loose feathers, in many cases both natural and dyed.

Ornamental Plumes; Herl: Whenever the barbs of a feather are soft and/or widely spaced apart, with relatively few barbules and no barbicels, the result is what we call "fluff" or "down." Most of the feathers used to tie flies have some barbs of this type near the butt of the quill; those called **plumes** are almost entirely "fluffy." Sometimes, as with marabou, even the central quill is soft and pliable. Because of this, both the entire plume and barbs stripped from the quill are variously used to tie flies.

Several types of plumes besides marabou are used in fly tying. The widely separated, very long and limber barbs of ostrich and peacock plumes are called **herl.** The barbules of herl appear as "feathery" fringes along both sides of the barb. The barbules of peacock herl also reflect light in iridescent colors ranging from brownish-gold to greenish-gold. Herl is an absolutely first-class material for many fly tying applications. It's used for everything from wrapping fly bodies to forming the overwings of wet fly and streamer patterns. Very green peacock herl is an especially good choice for the upper body/wing material on saltwater streamers and bucktails.

Plumage is sold as loose feathers. Peacock herl is also available in clusters of stripped barbs.

Near the tip of the peacock's tail plume the barbs touch with lapping barbules to form a characteristic "eye," called **peacock eye.** When these barbs are trimmed from the quill and stripped of barbules the barbs are usually light colored on one side, dark on the other. This feature, together with the long tapering shape of the barb makes stripped peacock eye quill an ideal material for dry fly and other fly bodies. When tied in by the tip and wrapped closely along the shank of the hook the result is a segmented body that looks like that of an insect, such as a mosquito, mayfly or caddis. The stripped central quill of hackle feathers such as the grizzly hackle can also be used to achieve a similar effect.

Miscellaneous Feathers. There are so many kinds of feathers used to tie flies — indeed, so many different kinds of birds whose feathers *could* be used in fly tying — that to describe them all is not practical. In fact, that's not really the point of this book. Once you've been able to visualize just what a feather is comprised of and how the relatively few standard types can be used to tie flies you'll easily recognize the possible uses for any feather from any source.

Still, I think it wise to alert you to some of the other feathers you'll be using sooner or later. For instance, turkey wing and tail feathers are used in the same ways as primaries and secondaries of waterfowl; that is, sections of barbs are trimmed and used for the wings of hopper patterns,

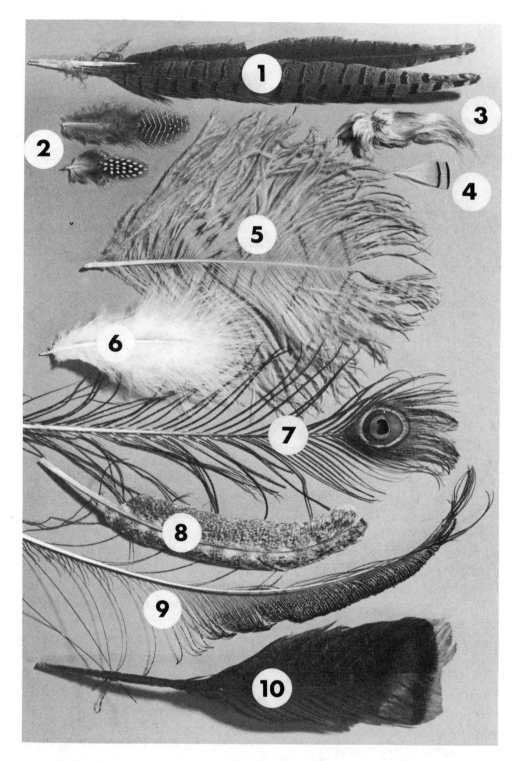

Figure 14. ORNAMENTAL PLUMES AND MISCELLANEOUS FEATHERS. (1) Paired ringneck pheasant tail, (2) two types of guinea fowl, (3) golden pheasant crest and (4) tippet, (5) dyed ostrich herl, (6) marabou plume, (7) peacock tail with "eye" and attached herl, (8) turkey wing, (9) peacock "sword", and (10) dyed turkey tail.

streamers and so on. The tail feather barbs of pheasants can be used to wrap the bodies of small nymphs. The crest feathers of the golden pheasant are used in streamer type flies, while its neck hackles, called tippets, are used in such flies as the Royal Coachman. Peacock sword is very effectively used in one saltwater streamer fly and has other applications, of course. Guinea fowl has wide application in nymph patterns and wet flies. Figure 14 will help you to recognize some of the feathers I've discussed. Most are sold as loose feathers, dyed or natural. Generally, only certain parts of each are used.

Sources and Substitutes. Most of the feathers you'll need can be purchased from fly materials dealers. If you're a hunter or have a friend who is, by all means save the feathers from wildfowl. You'll find that on today's market high quality feathers do not come cheap; as a rule the higher the quality, the higher the price you'll have to pay.

Some feathers that have been long standing favorites of the fly tier are now impossible to obtain. Jungle Cock, to name just one, is a totally protected bird whose exportation and importation is illegal. Several substitutes made of synthetic materials have been offered. The ones I've seen for the most part leave something to be desired. Perhaps in the future they'll improve. One, a recently introduced photo-dyed turkey feather is discussed in more detail under "New Products."

Other Non-metallic Fiber Materials

In addition to the different tying threads discussed earlier, many kinds of natural and man made fiber or fiber-like materials are used to tie flies. Some are metallic or appear to be made of metal; others are not. Some are stranded while others consist of a single continuous fiber or narrow ribbon. Representative of the common non-metallic fiber materials used in fly tying are those shown in Figure 15.

Floss. Fly tying floss is a lustrous flat thread-like material made of silk or any of several synthetic fibers such as nylon and rayon. It's sold on the spool, on cards and on large cones. Skeined floss, such as the type sold in sewing shops is a twisted strand floss and is not suited to fly tying unless the fibers are untwisted, generally not worth the trouble. Flat floss is preferred because it does not build up as rapidly, making it a lot easier to form a smooth well-shaped fly body. Some kinds of floss are more difficult to tie with than others; silk, for example, must be handled carefully as it tends to stick to rough spots on your fingers. Sometimes floss has a tendency to pull apart while the fly is being tied. In my experience, practice is the only solution to this problem. Sometimes a tier will wind the floss over a coat of head cement applied to the hook. This is a perfectly acceptable way to form the body. Don't, however, make the mistake of applying the cement directly on to the floss; I've found it invariably weakens the floss, causing it to pull apart.

Fly tying flosses are available in a very good selection of colors, dyed with both regular and radiant (fluorescent) dyes.

Yarns. Many types of yarn, made of both natural and synthetic fibers, are used to tie flies. Yarns made of natural hairs such as **wool** and **mohair** have been used to dress flies for a very long time and are superb in patterns where their water absorbency is desired. But you'll find that in many applications some of the new synthetics exhibit superior qualities. One, **polypropylene**, is a notably non-water absorbent fiber which makes it particularly suited to a wide variety of dry fly applications. Another is **acrylic.** Acrylic fibers have a gloss and brilliance that come to life in the water. Acrylics are also the closest thing to the old standby wool yet offered.

Yarn Tye, a thick loosely stranded cord comprised of acrylic fibers, is not a yarn in the true sense of the word. It's made for gift wrapping purposes and comes in white and a

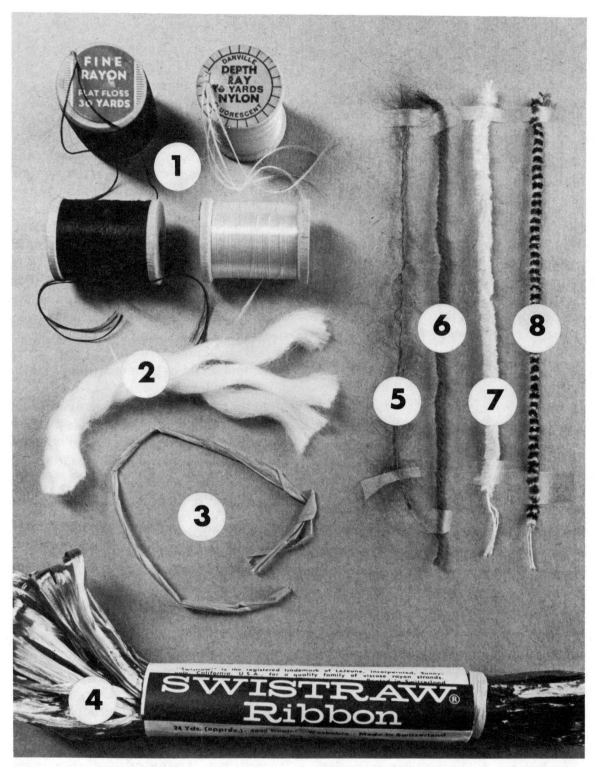

Figure 15. OTHER NON-METALIC FIBER MATERIALS. Typical examples include: (1) plain and radiantly dyed spooled unwaxed nontwisted floss; (2) acrylic "Yarn Tye"; (3) natural raffia; (4) viscose rayon "Swisstraw" ribbon; (5) mohair and (6) wool yarns; and (7) large diameter plain and (8) small diameter variegated chenille.

limited selection of primary, bright colors. However, it is used to pad or wrap some large fly bodies and for other applications. It has a tendency to pull apart when stretched. You can obtain Yarn Tye in the greeting card and gift wrapping sections of many stores.

Yarns are available in nearly any color, shade and size the tier needs. The types most suited to tying flies are stocked by the various fly materials dealers; some may be found in commercial yarn shops.

Chenille. Chenille is an excellent material for fly bodies. It is manufactured by twisting hair or hair-like fibers between two strands of thread — or in some cases, wire. The fibers extend through the twisted core at right angles for an equal distance each side. The result is a dense, furry cord that resembles the body of a caterpillar; indeed, the word chenille means *caterpillar* in French.

Chenilles are made from a variety of fibers, sometimes a mixture of different types and colors. The best chenilles for fly tying are made of nylon and other synthetics. Silk Chenille is also made, but it tends to rapidly lose brilliance in water. Some chenilles are made with a tinsel strand running along the core that adds sparkle to the fly's body. Wire chenille is a type of chenille made with a twisted wire core. One common example of this type of chenille is the "furry" cleaner pipe smokers use to clean their pipes. Wire chenille made with brass wire is suited to tying certain kinds of flies where corrosion resistance and durability are needed.

Chenille is available in a full range of fly tying colors and sizes, including brilliantly dyed colors. You'll find chenille difficult to obtain except through fly materials dealers.

Raffia. This is the wide, flat fiber from the raffia palm tree. It comes in natural and dyed colors. Soaked in water, then tied in place it's used to form overbodies, nymphal wingcases and the bodies of sinking flies. It is an opaque, very durable material.

Swisstraw. This material is a synthetic, a translucent viscose rayon ribbon that when soaked in water and tied in place makes an excellent substitute for raffia. It was originally manufactured to be used as decorative gift wrapping twine. It comes in a wide range of pastel shades. Swisstraw is not as strong or durable as raffia. It should be coated, after tying in place, with a clear head cement or epoxy.

Monofilament. Nylon monofilament is another synthetic fiber used to tie flies. As fishing line, it is available in a wide range of diameters (depending upon line strength) from very fine to coarse. It is produced in both round (circular cross-section) and oval shapes, and in several shades of color. Monofilament readily accepts dyes and can be either vat dyed or tinted with some types of waterproof felt marking pens, before or after tying the fly.

Nylon monofilament is used for ribbing, body, and tail construction. Wrapped as a solid body, it closely simulates the segmented bodies of insects, especially when oval monofilament is employed. Monofilament is a dense and heavy material, not ideally suited to dry fly construction.

Metal and Metalized Materials

Many fly patterns call for the use of metallic or metallic appearing materials to form bodies, parts of wings and what is known as the **rib** and **ribbing**. Ribbing is simply any distinctly contrasting thread-like material spirally wrapped along the body of the fly, usually to promote a segmented effect. Several types of materials are used to perform these functions. Figure 16 presents representative examples of metallic type materials used to tie flies.

Tinsel. One of the standard types is called **tinsel**, a gold or silver plated metal tape, ribbon or cord. To be nontarnishing, the plating must be done over a brass, copper or nickel-silver base. Tinsel is made in several sizes, some very small in diameter or width. It comes in flat, oval and

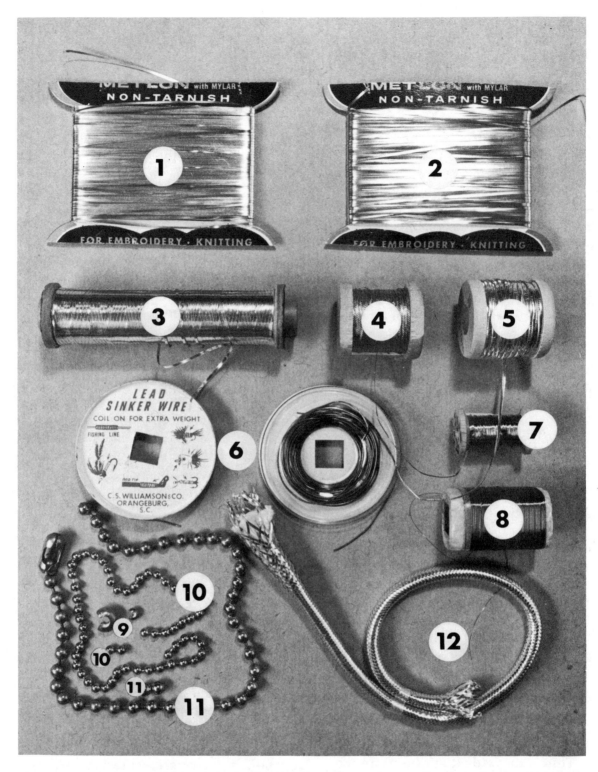

Figure 16. METAL AND METALIZED MATERIALS. Typical examples include: carded (1) gold and (2) silver mylar; (3) spooled silver (or gold) mylar; (4) spooled gold (or silver) flat tinsel; (5) spooled silver oval tinsel; (6) lead wire; (7) gold wire; (8) fine copper (transformer) wire; (9) brass split beads; (10) small chromed bead chain; and (12) silver mylar tubing (piping).

round types. Some tinsels are smooth; others have an embossed surface that catches more light than the smooth kinds. Wire tinsels not only make good ribbing material but help to hold the fly together, making for a much more durable product.

Mylar. This is a tinsel-like material that has now earned a lasting place in fly tying. It's available on spools and cards in silver, gold and other colors. Mylar (often referred to as "mylar tinsel") differs from true tinsel in that it is plated on plastic tape. It is not as strong as good tinsel, but it's easier to use and performs as well or better for most applications. Mylar does not tarnish, making it an ideal material for tying saltwater patterns.

Mylar Tubing (also called **Piping**). This is another useful form of mylar that consists of strands of mylar (gold or silver) braided around a heavy cotton core. When the core is removed the remaining braided shell or tube makes an ideal body for certain types of streamer flies and bucktails. The braided surface gives the appearance of the scales on the sides of baitfish. Light is reflected in all directions, adding a sparkly look to the fly's body. When the individual strands of mylar tubing are separated they retain a kinky shape. Added to the wings or topping of bucktails and streamers they provide the extra "flash" that often makes the fly more attractive to fish. Some mylar tubings are tightly braided, others are not. This creates a problem: when cut into lengths, the loosely braided types tend to unravel at the ends. You can avoid this by applying a ring of head cement where you intend to cut. The dried cement will hold the severed strands in position.

Mylars and tinsel are available from fly materials dealers. Mylar strands and tubings can occasionally be found in stores that stock notions and sewing supplies.

Wire. Small diameter wire of brass, copper and other metals are used to rib fly bodies. Whatever type is used should be made of a metal that will not corrode, or if it does it should

tarnish very slowly. Aluminum wire especially should never be used for saltwater flies, if indeed at all. Gold wire is absolutely non-corrodible, but of course it's also more expensive. Wires of the types most commonly used in fly tying can be obtained from fly materials dealers. Fine copper wire can be obtained from stranded electrical wiring and from discarded copper-wound transformer coils.

Stainless steel wire is also used in fly tying, principally in the construction of tandem hooked flies and wiggle-legged bass bugs.

Lead wire is used to weight the bodies of flies to make them sink. Lead wire comes in several sizes including Extra Fine (.010 diameter), Fine (.017 diameter), Medium (.026 diameter) and Heavy (.032 diameter). Lead wire for fly tying purposes is buss fuse wire. Very fine diameter soldering wire can be used but it's more brittle and, if resin cored, may result in undesirable staining of the finished fly.

Bead Chain. This is the same bead chain used for venetian blind pull cords, key chains and other purposes. It comes in sizes 3, 6 and 10; silver in all three sizes, gold in No. 6 only. Cut off in pairs with a pair of sidecutters, bead chain may be tied in place with a "figure eight" knot as buggy eyes for shad flies and other streamers. Such eyes are both effective and durable.

Split Beads. Split beads are small hollow light weight brass spheres cut nearly in half that come with the two halves pried open. When the split bead is clamped together over wrapped padding saturated with head cement, or filled with an easy-melt metal available for the purpose, it forms a smooth bulbous head or segmented body on the fly. The bead may be left natural or painted to suit. Split beads are made in ⅛ and ¼ inch diameters.

Elastomeric and Buoyant Materials

Elastomerics are materials that when stretched and released return to essentially their original sizes and shapes. Natural rubber is one

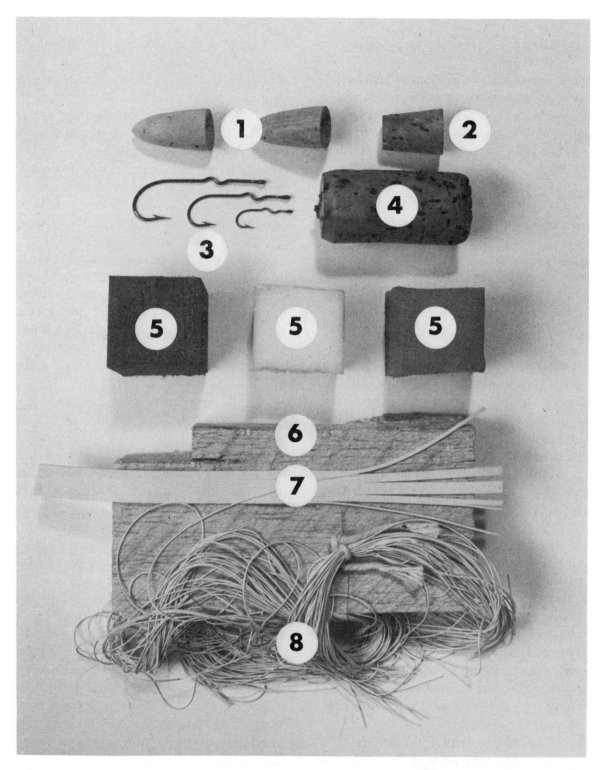

Figure 17. ELASTOMERIC AND BUOYANT MATERIALS. Some of the typical materials used in the construction of surface popping bugs include: (1) preformed concave faced popper corks; (2) standard cork bottle stopper; (3) kinked shank popper hooks; (4) wine bottle cork; (5) low density fine closed cell foam ("Evazote" or polyethylene in white and colors); (6) balsa wood; (7) peel off type rubber hackle; and (8) small size stranded soft rubber hackle.

example of such a material; many synthetic products also possess this ability. **Buoyant** materials are natural or synthetic substances that for one reason or another will float. Some are naturally lighter (less dense) than water; others entrap air so that the volume of material plus trapped air weighs less than an equal volume of water. Thus, like a boat built of metal heavier than water or the air filled cells within a chunk of volcanic pumice rock, the mass rides on the water's surface. Some elastomeric materials are buoyant. Many naturally buoyant materials, such as deer body hair and balsa wood exhibit no elastomeric qualities at all.

Rubber in the form of strips and sheets is not buoyant. Unless it is produced as an entirely closed cell foam — either from natural latex or a plastic such as urethane — it will simply act as a sponge and sink. Soft rubber type foams are usually not suitable for use where a fly is intended to float. However, rubber is often utilized in conjunction with other buoyant materials, chiefly in the form of "rubber hackle" (see Figure 17) and latex sheeting.

Rubber Hackle. Rubber hackle is the term given to a type of very soft and flexible natural latex rubber that comes in both precut loose fibers and live rubber sheets precut for easy separation. One can separate the hackle into the widths one chooses. Rubber hackle is available in both black and white. Its primary use is to form the legs on popping bugs.

Latex Rubber Sheeting. Latex sheeting is a relatively new material that is gaining wide favor among fly tiers. It is also known as "dental dam" because it was first used and still is in the field of dentistry. It is an excellent material for the bodies of shrimp, scud, nymphs, caddis and similar patterns where a comparitively tough, resilient and lifelike imitation of the body casing is desired. Latex comes as a thin, very soft and pliable sheet material. It must be cut into narrow strips for use. It is usually wrapped over an underbody. The same material can be obtained by cutting strips from thin surgical rubber gloves. It may be used "as is" (natural cream color) or dyed. An effective way to color latex is by using waterproof marking pens.

Cork. Cork is the bark of the cork oak tree. It is a longtime standard in fly tying because of its excellent floating qualities and durability. It is very easy to work into shape and retains its buoyancy even when coated with a variety of paints. Cork is primarily used for the bodies of bass and other types of popping bug patterns. Good cork is tight grained, with a minimum of voids and surface pits. I suggest you save your wine bottle corks; they're usually of fine quality and ample size for making flies. Ordinary bottle stopper corks can be obtained from variety and hardware stores, but they are not always of the best quality and must be carefully chosen. Pre-shaped popper corks in several different sizes are available from fly materials dealers. Fill the holes and surface pits in inferior corks with plastic wood after shaping, then sand and paint.

Balsa Wood. This is another natural product used for popper bodies. Balsa is a light and highly buoyant wood with a smooth close-grained structure. It normally lacks the pits and holes associated with cork. It can be easily cut, shaped, sanded, glued and painted. Balsa makes a relatively durable fly body. It is sold in a variety of sizes in hobby stores and occasionally in other retail outlets.

Foamed Plastics. Today, thanks to chemistry, many types of plastic foams are available, manufactured from a wide range of synthetic compounds. A few have already been used with varying success to tie flies. Others await the imaginative fly tier.

There are many different types of foam. Even foams made from the same plastic base often differ in their physical properties. Density, texture, resilience, compressibility, durability, water repellence, color and other factors can even be tailored to suit specific applications. However, a great many standard types have already been developed for industry and some of these specialized foam products are readily available to the fly tier; others are still hard or costly to obtain. Of course, with any manufactured material, supply usually responds to demand. Even the purely industrial high technology foams will become available when enough fly tiers demand a source.

Plastics are foamed to produce either **open cell** or **closed cell** structures. The end products range from the soft open cell kitchen sponge that absorbs water and sinks, to the rigid closed cell highly buoyant "Styrofoam" cup. In general, open cell foams tend to absorb water and sink, or at best become waterlogged and heavy. The type of urethane foam rubber used in mattresses is an example. This type, trimmed into thin narrow strips, is sometimes wrapped on the hook to form a padded underbody for sinking patterns. Many rigid foams are light and extremely buoyant but they too often lack the workability or durability desired in fly construction.

Closed cell foams range from rigid to very soft. As a general rule, such foams are buoyant substances. Some have minimal water repellency and will eventually sink; others are highly non-absorptive and will float indefinitely. Some are durable and tough; others, such as the familiar styrene type ("Styrofoam," for example) are soft, crumbly and not of much use as a fly tying material. The rigid foam used for Christmas decorations can be formed into popping bug bodies, but it is only minimally durable and sometimes difficult to finish to a smooth surface. A few foams, such as neoprene, are non-buoyant despite having closed cell structures. Some closed cell types float well enough, but are either too soft or tend to tear easily. Other compressible types have slow rates of recovery and may even retain surface indentations permanently. Some foams do not accept colored dyes or paints well, or at all.

Thus, when the standard foams are examined with an eye to their fly tying potential, most exhibit one or more undesirable traits. On closer inspection, many, but not all, seem to be entirely unsuited to fly construction. Several offer real possibilities, and two kinds of closed cell foams,

if not already in use by fly tiers, should be. One of the two, in my opinion, comes closest of all to qualifying as the "ideal" fly body material for floating patterns. Because these foams appear to be virtually unknown, I've elected to introduce two types as "new products" in the discussion that follows.

New Products

Evazote.* My choice for the "ideal" buoyant body material. An imported, low density, very fine-textured closed cell ethylene vinyl acetate patented foam made for a variety of industrial applications. To my knowledge, I am the first to use the material to tie flies. **Evazote** is extremely lightweight, compressible and resilient, elastic, tough and water resistant. Bass bugs made of this material feel "alive." **Evazote** permanently bonds to itself after the application of moderate heat to both surfaces (using a warm iron, for example). It can also be bonded to itself or other materials using two-part epoxy (the 5 minute clear type works fine). **Evazote** may be cut with a sharp razor blade or trimmed to shape with fly tying scissors — even sanded to shape with a powered sander. It is available in white, grey, blue and orange. **Evazote** also accepts waterproof inks and dyes, offering wide latitude to the tier in tailoring the fly's color scheme to suit. It comes in a variety of strip and sheet sizes. For fly construction, a supply of 1"x1" strip is all you need. For the present, **Evazote** and similar foams remain difficult for the tier to obtain in small quantities. Some of the currently authorized distributors are listed under "Sources."

Polyethylene (Polythene) Foams. A whole family of foams, the best of which are in my opinion second only to *Evazote* as buoyant body materials. The fine textured cross-linked polyethylene closed cell foams such as the

*Trademark of Bakelite Xylonite Limited

36

Minicel series and **Plastizote** offer nearly all of the advantages of *Evazote* — workability, bondability, compressibility, coloring capability and buoyancy. However, they may not be quite as tough, durable and resilient. Some I've tried appear to retain surface indentations indefinitely. Polythene closed cell foams are produced in many different shapes, sizes, densities and colors. The best quality foams are designed for industrial use and, like *Evazote*, are not offered for sale through retail sources. Readily available polythene foams, such as the coarser textured foam used in weatherstripping, can be substituted but, depending upon the pattern, quality, durability and appearance may suffer.

Overton's Wonder Wax. This magnetic-adhesive fly tying wax is a big improvement over traditional dubbing waxes. A wax that sticks only when and where you need it — on the thread. No more messy fingers. Comes in a handy adjustable tube with cap that's used like the familiar dispenser for chapped lips. Available from fly materials dealers.

Poul Jorgensen's Seal-X; Mickey Powell's Seal-Lite; Kaufmann's Imitation Seal's Fur. Some of the recently introduced synthetic "seal furs." The animal itself is now on the Endangered Species List and genuine seal can no longer be legally collected. None of the imitations have the natural translucence of the real thing, but they make acceptable substitutes. All come in a good selection of colors. Obtainable from various fly materials sources.

Swannundaze. Another new product ideal for tying natural appearing nymph bodies, and for ribbing. A flat, oval plastic that's very soft, feels real and is much wider than the oval monofilament often used for the same purpose. Easy to work with. Available in 23 colors from the usual fly materials sources.

Flame Wing Cutter. A new, all metal wing making tool that comes in a set of four different sizes from large to fine to accommodate flies size 10 to 22. To make a perfectly formed wing every time, simply place a feather between the cutter's metal ends, squeeze and use a butane lighter to burn away the exposed feather. Brush the singed edges with your finger and you're ready to tie in the wing. The butane lighter is not included. Available from the usual fly materials sources.

Pantone Waterproof Marking Pens. A product of Letraset originally developed for the graphic arts field. Available in several marking point designs from wide to fine point. Very useful for creatively marking feathers, latex, foams and other materials. Indelible dyes are waterproof; however, liquid-type dry fly floatant solutions may dissolve or bleach the colors. Available in a wide range of colors and shades from both fly materials sources and graphic arts dealers.

Foto-Feathers. A unique replacement for the increasingly scarce mottled brown turkey feathers. A special photo-silk-screening process is used to imprint the natural brown feather color and markings on white turkey feathers. The result is a very effective imitation. The barbs on both sides of the quill are printed, offering twice the yield of the natural feather. Packaged in pairs. Available from River Systems.

Techniques

IV
Tips & Basic Tying Techniques

TIPS

To tie a fly, any fly, involves fastening various materials to the hook in ways that will result in a desired finished appearance. A few very special patterns accomplish this solely by the use of glue-type bonders; others, such as cork-bodied poppers, call for specific parts of the fly to be bonded into place. The vast majority of flies, however, are constructed by the time honored method of "tying" the fly; that is, the materials are bound to the hook with wraps of thread and finished with some sort of knot. Different effects are achieved by varying the ways the materials are wrapped with the thread.

This chapter will help you learn the relatively few basic techniques you'll need to know in order to construct not only the fly patterns in the next chapter, but most flies you'll wish to tie.

From here on you will be concentrating on the actual tying process. Some techniques will come easy, others will be more difficult to master. Believe me when I say that none of the techniques in this book are too hard for you. You'll need to practice, that's true. But with practice each technique will become easier and easier until you will be performing the tying process automatically. Your goal should be to reach the point where you can fully concentrate on the product, not the process. And the quickest way is through a slow, deliberate and systematic approach. Don't rush. In fact, I strongly advise you to study this chapter thoroughly before lifting a tool, then skim through the fly patterns in Chapter V and read the rest of the book. Become familiar with the first four plates in the Appendix dealing with fly parts and proportions. Build a picture in your mind of the tying process in general, of how the parts of a fly relate to each other, and how the techniques can be combined in various ways to achieve a

desired result. When you have done this, it will then be time to actually learn the techniques. Master each technique in Chapter IV before proceeding to the next. And because flies are constructed by several different techniques in combination, I emphasize: **practice all of them as individual skills before trying to tie a complete fly**. You will find this approach to fly tying will shorten learning time, help you to develop better habits and save money in the long run. You can reuse many of the practice materials and, in some cases, use practice materials of lesser quality.

Now, assuming you have followed my advice and are ready to begin learning the fly tying process, here are a few very important things to do:

1. Pre-plan your work area for comfort and convenience. Select a place to tie flies that affords enough space to hold all of the tools, materials and other items you'll be using. Make sure that the bench or table surface is elevated a comfortable height from the floor, and choose a comfortable chair in which to sit. Select a bench/chair combination that will allow you to sit erect while tying, but one in which the vise jaws are located well above the bench or table surface. You need ample clearance to work the bobbin. Spending the time to determine the right heights for you can spell the difference between a pastime of pleasure or one of nagging pain. Poor tying posture often leads to problems with neck or back.

2. Arrange all tools and materials for easy access. Here's where a little thought and planning really pays off. Make sure that your fly tying vise is firmly clamped to the bench or table and that its jaws are positioned at the correct height above the surface. Be wise: take the time to study the clamping mechanism of the vise you're using so you fully understand how to adjust it properly. Many students experience unnecessary difficulty, even damage their vises, because they won't take time to study the vise's operation.

Arrange or place the various tools and materials roughly in the order in which they will be needed. Include a note pad and pen or pencil to jot down notes. Keep a small scale or ruler handy.

Speaking of the need for a scale or ruler: let's discuss right here one of the most important considerations in fly tying — the need for you to develop your sense of proportion. That should be one of your ultimate goals: to be able to "feel" the correct fly proportions. Most people have the ability to learn to gauge by sight whether a material or fly part is too long, too short, too bulky or too sparse, or is wrongly oriented in relation to the other parts of the fly. Often, it's just a matter of learning to trust your own instinctive sense that something "looks right." As a beginner, measuring the parts as you apply each one in turn to the hook can help you to recognize the correct proportions for the fly pattern you're tying. Later, you may not need to measure a thing. Another aid in learning the standard proportions is to affix index tabs to the pages in the Appendix for Plates 2 and 3; in fact, it's a good idea to use index tabs for all pages containing information you will need to refer to on a repetitive basis.

3. Provide against accidents. When your full concentration is directed toward the fly you're tying, it's all too easy to tip over an open bottle of head cement or thinner. Head cement seems invariably to come in a bottle too tall and narrow for its base. When spilled, it makes a nasty mess.

One good way to avoid the problem is to make a stable base for the bottle from a block of rigid plastic foam, the type readily obtainable in most variety stores. Cut a hole in the center to snugly fit the base of the bottle. Plastic foam of this type can be used for other uses as well, including a convenient stand upon which to stick your finished flies.

Another way to circumvent the disaster of nasty spilled liquids is as follows: bond any small, flat permanent magnet to the bottom of the bottle using epoxy glue. A type of magnet well suited to the purpose is the kind made of vinyl plastic impregnated with magnetic material. Such magnets can usually be found in one shape or another in variety, hardware or similar stores. You may have to trim the magnet to fit the base of the bottle you're using, in which case the vinyl type is even better. Carry a small piece of flat sheet metal (either steel or iron or it won't work) in your kit. A piece about 3 inches square will do. This will provide a stable base for the bottle (or bottles) while you're tying, yet the weak magnetic bond can be easily broken when necessary.

If you are a cigarette smoker, use the type of ashtray designed to trap a forgotten burning cigarette. When your concentration is fully directed toward the fly you're working on, it's all too easy to forget. At the very least, the result can be a burned bench or table top.

4. Provide proper illumination. Make sure the work area is well illuminated and that you have plenty of light to see what you're doing. If possible, spotlight the fly from an indirect light source located so that you receive none of the glare.

Provide a light toned background behind the fly held in the vise. A piece of white or off-white cardboard will serve. A light, bland background makes it much easier to visually define the fly and each of its component parts.

Keep a small mirror handy, preferably of the magnifying type. You will find this a valuable aid in checking the back of the fly you're tying, especially if your vise is the kind that does not swivel. You should always make certain the fly is being tied symmetrically; when finished, both sides should match.

5. Read all instructions beforehand. Before you plunge ahead and start tying a fly, take the time to completely read through the instructions for tying that particular pattern. Make sure you have all of the materials called for and that you fully understand the tying steps and techniques you will need to perform. I can readily understand and sympathize with the impatient student, eager to get started, but I've found that an orderly and systematic approach to any problem, including tying flies, usually results in a better product. After you have tied a particular fly, don't assume you've mastered it until you've tied at least *six* more just like it. Class experience has shown that only after a student has tied six or more flies of the same pattern is he or she ready to move on to the next one.

And now, with that bit of advice, you're ready to move on to the actual tying process.

Basic Tying Techniques

All tied flies have two things in common: they start with one kind of knot and end with another. The knot used to start the fly is called a **jamb knot**; the knot most commonly used to finish off the fly is called the **whip finish**. Some tiers use another type of knot called the **half-hitch** to finish the fly, but for reasons to be explained later, the whip finish knot is a much better way to finish the fly. The half-hitch is more effectively used to secure each material during the tying process. In order to start and finish a fly you must be thoroughly familiar with how to tie both the jamb knot and whip finish. It's too late to learn once you've tied all of the materials into place. For that reason, before you attempt to tie a fly, I urge you to practice both knots until you can tie them with confidence.

1. Starting The Fly. To learn the basic techniques, it's wise to practice with a large sized stout wire hook and Size A tying thread. Not only can you see what you're doing better, but it's not so easy to break the thread — a

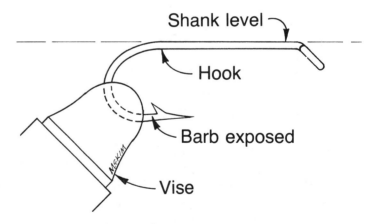

Figure 18. Proper vise/hook orientation.

frustrating and frequent occurrence among beginners.

Place the hook in your vise and clamp the jaws to hold it rigidly. The correct positioning of the hook in the vise is shown in Figure 18. Load the fly tying bobbin with a spool of tying thread and adjust it so the thread will release evenly under moderate tension. Some bobbins have a tensioning knob. If your bobbin is of the Matarelli type, tensioning can be accomplished in one of two ways: either spread the two legs apart or compress them together to accommodate the thread spool you're using, or simply allow one or more loops of thread to slip off to one side so the thread wraps around one leg. The resulting friction works beautifully as a tensioning adjustment.

2. Head Space. I cannot overemphasize the importance of leaving enough head space (Figure 19). Experience has shown this to be the single most common error of beginning

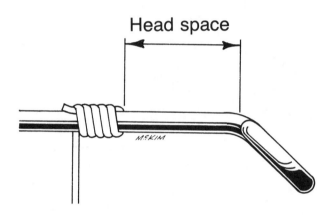

Head space

Figure 19. Head space.

students. Head space will vary with the fly pattern you're tying and with the size of the fly, but it serves two important functions: first, it's designed to allow the formation of a properly proportioned head and, second, it must be long enough to allow you to tie off and complete the fly. Because virtually all flies start near the head and end with the head, students tend to make the error of crowding the head space with each successive addition of material. At the end, they're in trouble. No room is left for the head of the fly. Try to develop the habit early — **leave head space!**

3. The Jamb Knot. Despite its name, the jamb knot is not a true knot in the strict meaning of the word. It's merely a means of binding the tying thread to the hook that allows a smooth, even start to the fly, without unwanted bulging and lumpiness. When thread is wrapped around a hook shank and over itself under tension, friction tends to bind it tightly in place, and so long as sufficient tension is maintained this friction also prevents the wraps from sliding around the shank. This is the principle of the jamb knot. If you release the tension, the knot immediately unwinds and comes apart. After you've formed the jamb knot, you must always keep the thread under tension. When you're not tying, let the bobbin hang freely. Its weight will provide enough tension on the thread to keep the knot intact.

Tying the Jamb Knot

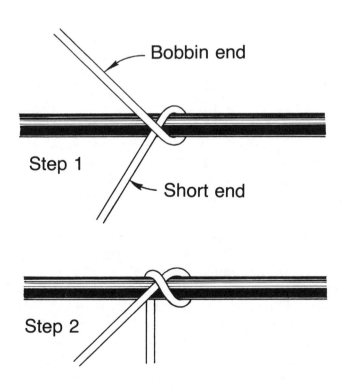

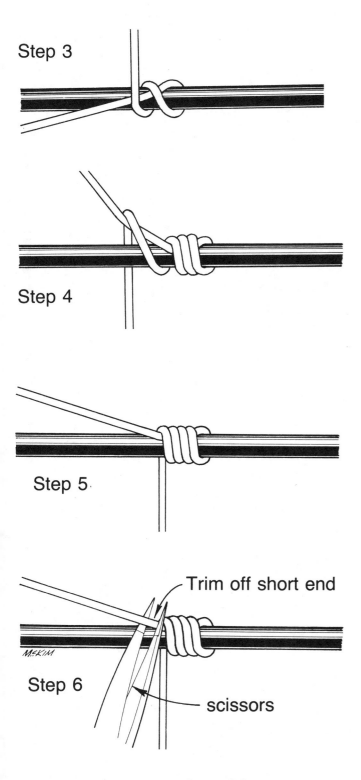

Step 3

Step 4

Step 5

Trim off short end

Step 6

scissors

M^cKIM

Figure 20. Tying the jamb knot.

Figure 20 illustrates the technique used to form the jamb knot. It must be done swiftly and smoothly using both hands as shown. A few minutes study and practice is usually all it takes to learn to tie it. After you've formed the knot, use your fingers to slide it along the hook's shank to its proper position behind the head space. Usually, three or four wraps are all that are required to form a stable jamb knot. You may then either trim off the loose end of the tying thread or tie it down with consecutive wraps as you proceed toward the bend of the hook. This makes a uniformly thick underwrapping of thread.

4. The Whip Finish. The whip finish is a true knot; that is, after the knot is formed and tightened, releasing the tension on the thread will not cause it to work loose. Among most fly tiers, it is the preferred method of finishing the fly. For two reasons: first, when it is correctly formed, the whip finish results in a smooth flat knot without bulges or lumps, and second, it allows you to precisely control the shape of the fly's head as it's being formed.

There are several different tools you can purchase through fly materials sources that are designed to help you tie the whip finish knot. If you feel you absolutely need a device to help you tie the knot, by all means buy one. In fact, one — the Matarelli Improved Whip Finisher — is an especially good tool for finishing the smaller sizes of flies in particular. However, the method illustrated in Figures 21 and 22 will allow you to do the same thing. All that's required for this technique are two hands, some study and practice. It may seem difficult at first, but with a little perserverance most people are able to master the so-called "two hand whip finish" in less time than they'd imagine. In deference to those of you who are "southpaws," both right and left-hand versions of the technique are shown.

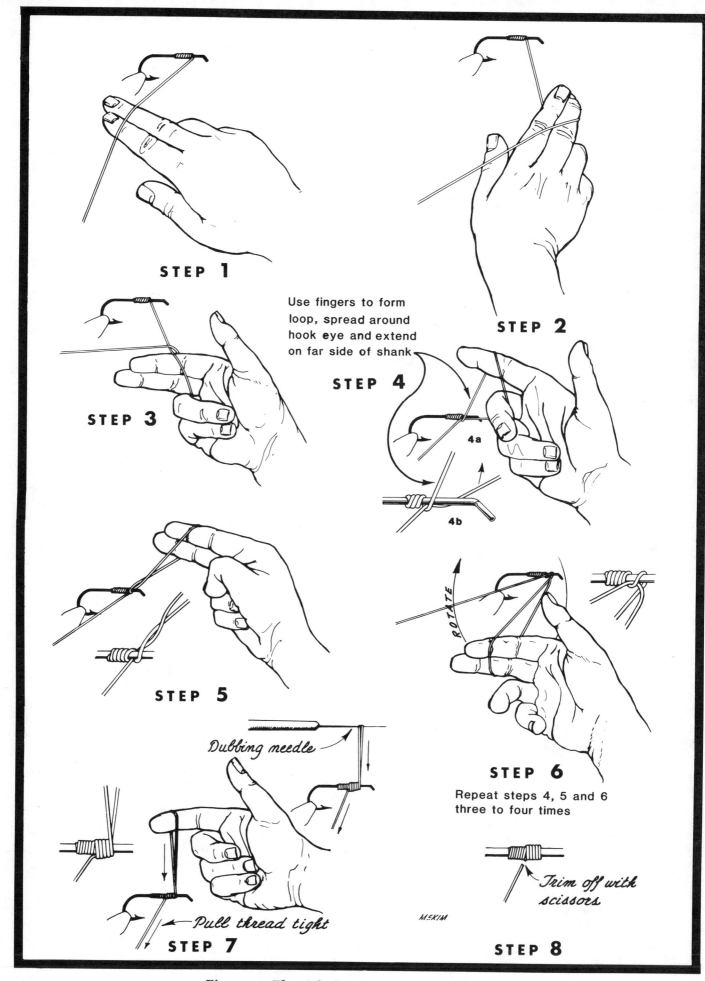

STEP 1

STEP 2

STEP 3

Use fingers to form loop, spread around hook eye and extend on far side of shank

STEP 4

4a

4b

STEP 5

ROTATE

STEP 6

Repeat steps 4, 5 and 6 three to four times

Dubbing needle

Pull thread tight

STEP 7

Trim off with scissors

STEP 8

M SKIM

46

Figure 21. The right-handed whip finish knot.

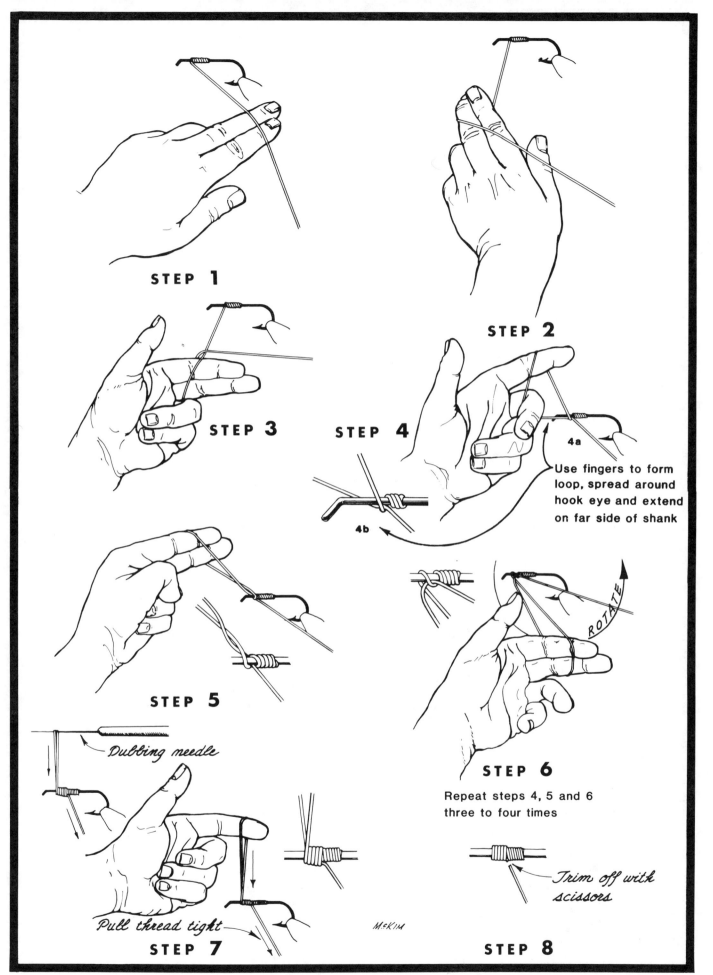

STEP 1

STEP 2

STEP 3

STEP 4

4a

Use fingers to form loop, spread around hook eye and extend on far side of shank

4b

STEP 5

ROTATE

STEP 6

Repeat steps 4, 5 and 6 three to four times

Dubbing needle

Pull thread tight

STEP 7

Trim off with scissors

STEP 8

McKIM

Figure 22. The left-handed whip finish knot.

47

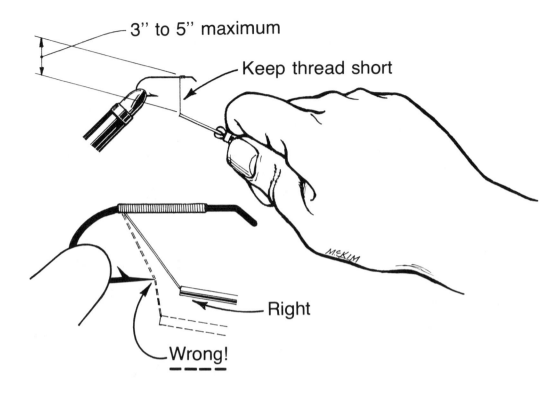

3" to 5" maximum

Keep thread short

Right

Wrong!

Figure 23. Correct use of the bobbin.

5. Correct Use Of The Bobbin. From the outset, you should develop the habit of holding and manipulating the bobbin, **never the thread** itself. The fly tying bobbin is designed to direct a continuous supply of thread toward the fly. And, it is much more than just an extension of your fingers; using a bobbin gives you pin-point control over the tying process. To exercise this control you should always maintain the shortest practicable length of thread between thread and bobbin during the tying process. This allows you to accurately position each succeeding thread wrap and, when wrapping near the bend of the hook, helps to avoid accidentally nicking the thread on the point. Even the smallest nick by the hook's point tends to weaken the tying thread; often the thread begins to unravel or actually break. Remember, always avoid the hook's point when tying.

Of course, there are many times when a short thread is not necessary, such as when the bobbin is allowed to hang freely while not in use, or when additional thread is required to tie in materials or form a whip finish or half-hitch. At all times during the wrapping process, however, try to keep the thread length between bobbin and fly relatively short, 3 to 5 inches; even shorter when necessary.

Figure 23 illustrates the correct way to hold the bobbin while tying.

6. The Half-Hitch Knot. As mentioned earlier, the half-hitch knot has been used by many fine fly tiers both to anchor succeeding steps of the fly and to finish the head of the fly. When properly used, the half-hitch is an excellent knot to use during the tying process. I recommend that you learn to tie the knot and apply it after each succeeding material is wrapped on the hook. This will make for a much more durable fly. However, a single half-hitch is not secure enough by itself to complete the fly. It will loosen if not well cemented in place. Several consecutive half-hitches are needed and by the time you've applied them it is usually quicker and easier to tie a whip finish. Besides, the whip finish offers much greater head forming control than is normally possible wth the half-hitch.

48

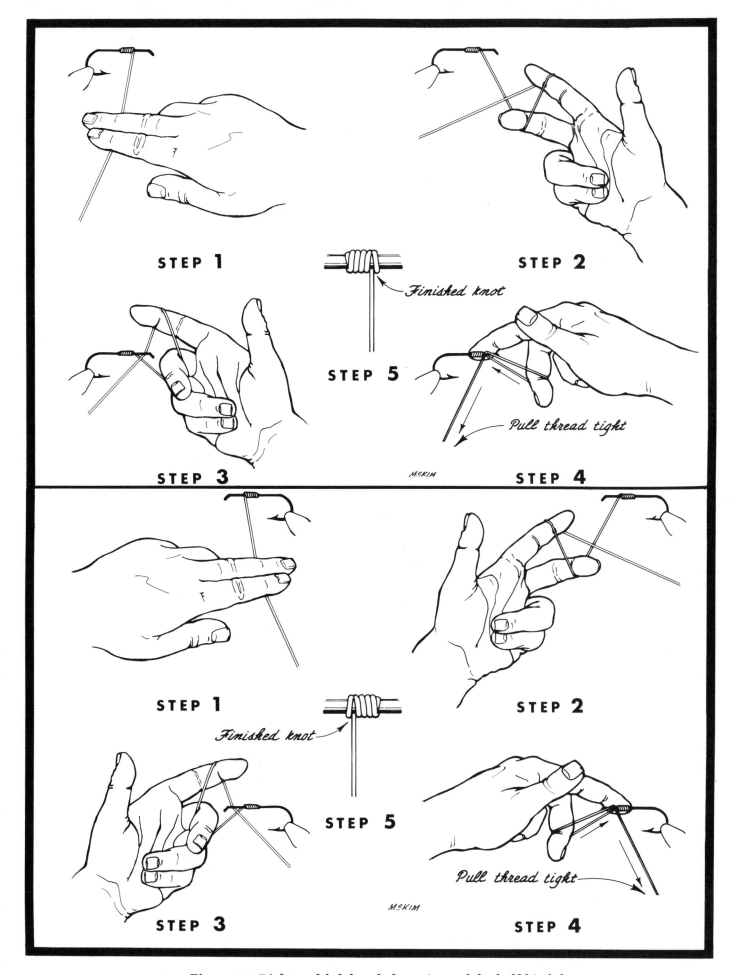

STEP 1

STEP 2

STEP 5 ← *Finished knot*

STEP 3

STEP 4 *Pull thread tight*

M°KIM

STEP 1

STEP 2

Finished knot → **STEP 5**

STEP 3

STEP 4 *Pull thread tight*

M°KIM

Figure 24. Right and left-handed versions of the half-hitch knot.

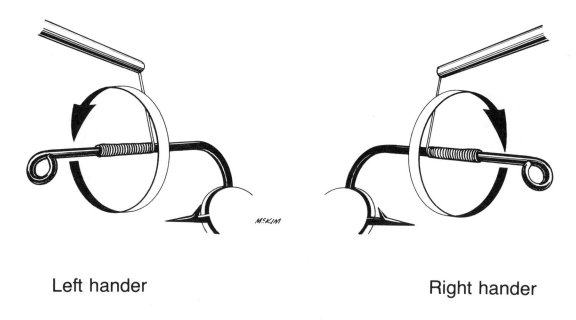

Left hander   Right hander

Figure 25. The correct wrapping technique.

There are several methods of tying the half-hitch. Figure 24 illustrates one very effective and easy technique for tying the knot. The method shown was first demonstrated to me by Grant Mounteer, a fine fly tier from California. I've used it ever since. A few minutes of study and practice are usually all that are required to learn the half-hitch. Again, both the right- and left-hand versions of the technique are shown for your convenience.

7. The Correct Wrapping Procedure. If you've studied the illustrations for the jamb and other knots, you will have already seen that in tying flies the tying thread is always wrapped up-away-down-toward the tyer. Put another way, if you look directly toward the eye of the hook in line with the shank, you will wrap the thread in a **clockwise** direction if you're **right-handed**, and in the **counterclockwise** direction if you're a **left-handed** person. Figure 25 illustrates the difference.

Throughout the tying of a fly you must always keep the thread ahead of each succeeding operation; that is, when you've finished securing a particular fly part, your last wrap of thread should be in position to apply the next part in the sequence. Each of the instructional fly patterns in the next chapter show and tell which

of the fly's parts are to be applied and the order in which each part occurs. As you become a more proficient fly tier, you will be able to look at a drawing or photograph of a complete fly and determine for yourself a logical order or sequence of steps in which it can be tied. Usually, there are at least two ways to construct a given fly. For consistency, all of the fly patterns in this book are shown starting immediately behind the head space. There are logical reasons for this: first, it immediately defines the important head space and constantly reminds the tier not to crowd it, and second, it helps to avoid unsightly bulging wraps of thread near the tail of the fly, bulges that become further accentuated when tail and body materials are subsequently applied.

8. Applying Materials In General. Obviously, to tie a fly you must be able to secure various kinds of materials on a hook. To do this involves wrapping the tying thread around both the shank and the material being tied on, then tightening the wraps to hold the material in place. Simple. Yet, this operation which appears so easy (and really is) seems to be difficult for many beginners to master. Often their confidence turns to dismay as one frustrating problem after another crops up. Either the

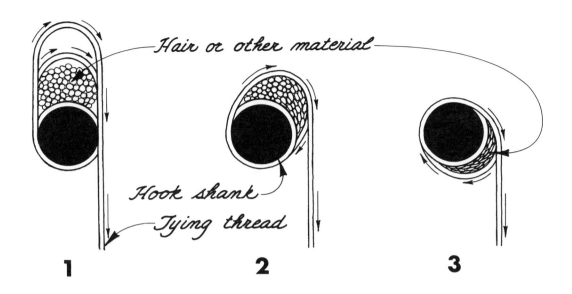

Figure 26. Without restraint, constricting wraps of tying thread act to roll materials around the hook's shank.

material is found to have rolled around the shank, or it is too loosely secured to maintain its position. The material may be tied in the wrong spot on the shank or the finished length may be shorter or longer than intended. Worse yet, the student may find himself the victim of several or all of the problems cited. These and other difficulties in fly tying are usually overcome with practice and an understanding of why each problem occurs.

Let's discuss each of the problems in turn. First, why does the material roll around the shank? To understand this, you must visualize the role of the thread itself. Figure 26 shows what happens as the tying thread is pulled and the wraps begin to constrict. The thread **moves** in the direction of pull, causing friction between the thread and material. As friction increases the thread wraps literally transport the material along in the direction of travel. This continues until the wraps are tight and the thread can no longer move. If sufficient pressure is applied to keep the material from moving, however, friction is overcome and the thread wraps **slide** over the material until tight. The solution, of course, is to apply just enough pressure to both the material and wraps of thread to prevent the material from moving, but not enough to completely bind the thread and cause it to break

from the strain. With practice the tier learns to apply just the right amount of pressure for the size thread he or she is using.

Figure 27 shows one method used by fly tiers to tie on those materials intended to remain in a specific location on the top, bottom or sides of the fly. The trick is to learn to **roll** the ends of your thumb and forefinger open and closed without relaxing pressure on the material while at the same time, gather the two loops of thread between them. Once you have the two loops of thread in position above the point at which you wish the material to be tied, pull straight down with the bobbin until the loops have constricted around the material. With practice, you'll soon learn to balance the pressure from your thumb and forefinger against the breaking limit of the tying thread. It's best to practice with heavier thread until you've mastered the technique. Remember, do not relax your grip until you're sure the wraps are tight: otherwise the material will immediately roll around the shank as soon as you apply the additional pressure needed to tighten the wraps. Of course, when you cannot add more tension to the tying thread (without breaking it), the material will remain securely in its proper position and the finished fly will be a durable product. No matter how the finished fly appears,

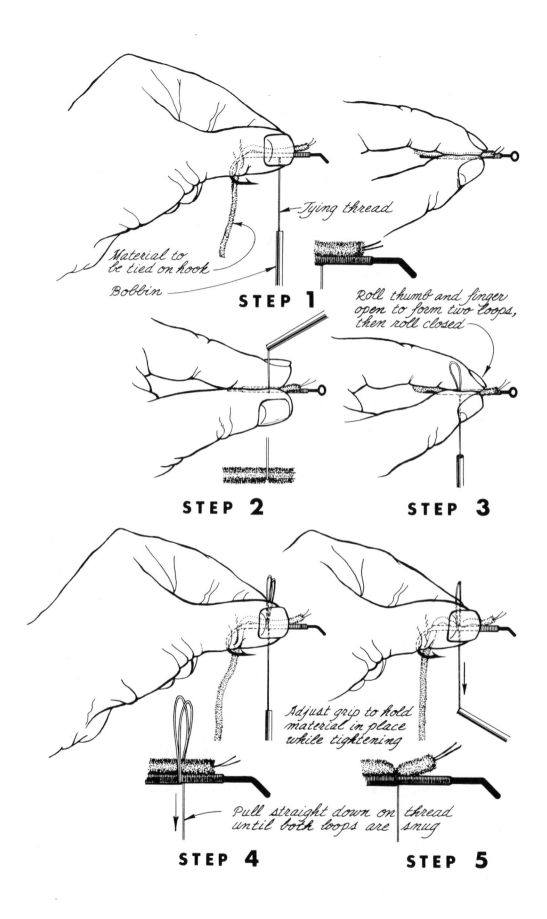

Figure 27. Basic technique used to apply a material to the hook.

if the wraps are not snug the fly will soon fall apart when used; a waste of effort.

Tying the material in the wrong place is another problem that is easily avoided if you make certain of two things: first, the bobbin must hang directly below the point at which you wish to tie in the material, and second, the two loops of thread shown in Figure 27 must be gathered together between thumb and forefinger directly above the same point. When the loops are in the correct position, pulling straight down on the thread will cause them to constrict together exactly where you intend the material to be secured.

When a specific length of material·is required in the finished fly — for example, a clump of hairs for the tail or wing — the material must be tied on at the precise point along its length that will result in a properly proportioned tail or wing once the butts are trimmed away. The best way to accomplish this is to grasp the butts with one hand, place the material atop the shank in the correct position (the bobbin must hang freely

below the point at which you plan to tie in the material, of course) and when you're sure the material is where you want it, transfer your grip to the opposite hand, then proceed to tie it down as shown in Figure 27.

With relatively solid materials such as hackle barbs and non-compressible types of hairs, it is possible to shorten or lengthen the material in place. To do this, proceed with the technique shown in Figure 27 but tighten the loops only enough to gently bind the material to the shank. Remove your hand and inspect the length. If the finished part will be too long, firmly grasp the end or ends of the material that will be trimmed away in the finished fly and pull the material through the thread wraps until the correct length is attained. If the material will be too short, reverse the process. Use a scale or ruler to make sure the length is correct. When you're satisfied, hold the material and firmly tighten it in place.

Shortening or lengthening the material this way does not work well when the material being tied on is a compressible substance, as for

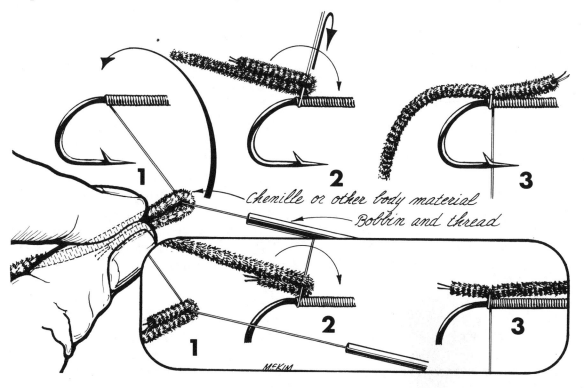

Figure 28. Alternate technique for applying strand-type materials to the hook.

53

example, deer body hair. If the initial wraps of thread are even moderately tight, the material deforms and it then becomes difficult or impossible to slide it backward or forward in an attempt to adjust to the desired length. When this happens, one is usually forced to unwrap the material and begin again. However, the fact that certain types of hairs tend to deform when tied down, and that unrestrained materials in general will roll around the shank is often used to advantage, as you shall see when I discuss the technique of spinning deer hair later in this chapter.

After any material is cinched down in the correct place on the hook, always apply several additional wraps of thread to make sure it remains in position. A half-hitch knot or drop of head cement at the point of connection will add some insurance.

The technique shown in Figure 27 may be used to tie all kinds of materials on to the hook; in fact, material such as "quill" wings **must** be tied on this way. But, there is an easier and simpler method that you can use to tie on yarns, chenille and similar stranded type materials used to form various parts of the fly's body. The technique shown in Figure 28 allows you to position the material exactly in the place it's needed without guesswork, and by choosing the direction it is wrapped around the thread, you can orient the butt end toward either the hook's eye or its bend.

9. Weighting the Body. Most fly types are "sinking" patterns meant to be fished at various levels of the water column. As such, they're usually constructed of water absorbent materials on heavier hooks to ensure they will sink. Combined with a sinking line and/or weighted leader, this is often all that is needed to reach the depth desired. But not always. Especially where the current is swift and deep. To get down and stay down, it's normal practice to add weight to the fly during the tying process. This can be done in several ways, two of which are illustrated.

Figure 29 shows a weighting technique commonly used to weight steelhead patterns and large nymphs. It offers several advantages. A smoother underbody can be formed and the method allows the tier to balance the fly and/or widen and flatten the body (for nymphs), depending upon how the lead is positioned in place. Regardless of the method used to add weight, the fly's sinking quality will depend upon the amount of wire, its diameter and the relative buoyancy of the other materials of which it's constructed.

Perhaps the most common method of weighting flies, especially small sizes, is the lead wire wrapping method shown in Figure 30. To apply lead weight by this technique, begin by wrapping the shank with tying thread. This forms a base. Let the bobbin hang behind where you intend to wrap the lead wire. Holding the end of the wire against the hook with your thumb, wrap the lead tightly around the shank with your free hand. When the desired number of wraps have been applied, pinch the wire in two with your thumbnail or clip with scissors. Bend the end down and compress the lead wraps together. They can usually be repositioned if required by pushing with your thumbnail. After the lead is in the correct place, secure it into position with tying thread as shown. Remember to always begin by bringing the thread forward across the full length of the thread and back. Repeat this several times before wrapping the tying thread more closely together. This helps to prevent the thread wraps from spreading the lead wire apart. When finished, coat the lead with head cement (or, in the case of dubbed fur bodies, with wax) prior to forming the body.

As you might suspect, after a fly is completed, it becomes very difficult, if not impossible, to determine whether or not it is weighted. Thus, it's a good idea to identify the weighted version as soon as it's finished. Choose any method you wish to differentiate between the weighted and non-weighted flies in your box. Some tiers have adopted the practice of tying the weighted version with a different (or distinctive) color of thread. The method I use and prefer is to paint a small dot of yellow or white lacquer atop the head of the weighted version. That way I can tell at a glance.

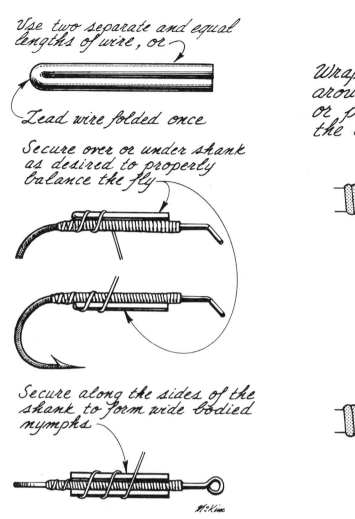

Use two separate and equal lengths of wire, or

Lead wire folded once

Secure over or under shank as desired to properly balance the fly

Secure along the sides of the shank to form wide bodied nymphs

McKim

Figure 29. Weighting the body by the bent wire method.

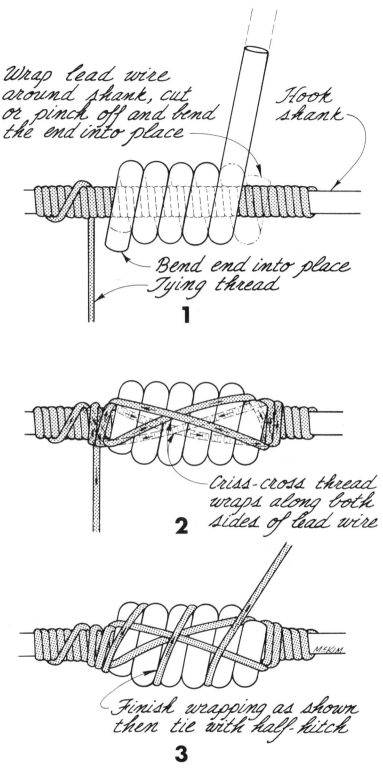

Wrap lead wire around shank, cut or pinch off and bend the end into place

Hook shank

Bend end into place
Tying thread

1

Criss-cross thread wraps along both sides of lead wire

2

Finish wrapping as shown then tie with half-hitch

3

Figure 30. Weighting the body by the wrapped wire method.

10. Wrapping Bodies. After the body material (or materials) has been tied in place (and the weighting has been applied, if it's a sinking pattern), wrap the tying thread forward to the point at which the fly's body will terminate. You're now ready to wrap the body, whether it's to be yarn, chenille or another strand-type material. To make the fly more durable, it's a good idea to coat the shank under the body with head cement prior to wrapping the body material into place. Before the cement has time to harden, wrap the body material closely around the shank as shown in Figures 31 and 32 until you reach the tying thread. Hold the body

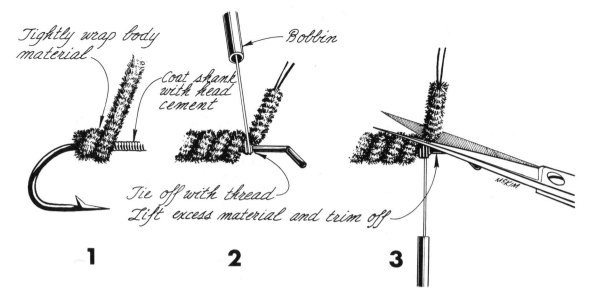

Tightly wrap body material

Coat shank with head cement

Bobbin

Tie off with thread
Lift excess material and trim off

1 **2** **3**

Figure 31. Wrapping the body

material snugly upright with your bobbin hand and lift the bobbin over with the other hand. Let it drop. Repeat this procedure at least one more time, then change hands and apply an extra wrap or two — or a half-hitch to make sure. Lift the loose body material vertically above the shank and trim it off close to the point of connection. **Never** trim away material (except the tying thread itself) below the shank when it's near the tying thread. Perhaps the most agonizing sound in a room full of beginning fly tiers is the report of a bobbin hitting the floor!

11. Dubbing. The technique of dubbing fly bodies, briefly defined in earlier chapters, is an excellent method of creating a fly body that combines both a certain amount of water-repellency and the "buggy" look so attractive to fish. It also affords the tier a great degree of flexibility. By varying the amount of dubbing material and its type, a body may be formed to virtually any shape and proportion one desires from fat to thin, tapered to cylindrical, relatively smooth to wildly fuzzy. Normally, bodies are dubbed to a uniform shade, but by varying the colors of the material you can make the body nearly any dark/light pattern you choose.

Dubbing material can be prepared in several ways. Underfur can be mixed together by hand or better still in a kitchen blender, a method particularly suited to the mixing together of furs from different animals and furs of various colors,

either natural or dyed. A high degree of homogeneity can be achieved using a blender. Simply trim the fur from the hide, place it in small amounts at a time in a blender set for high speed, and switch the machine on and off until the fur is blended to your satisfaction. You can remove the guard hairs before blending or leave them in, as you choose. If you don't have a blender, you can achieve essentially the same result by hand. Just take the underfur to be mixed, separate or "tease" the clumped hairs, then mix them together again. Repeat this "teasing and re-mixing" procedure until the dubbing mixture is thoroughly blended.

Figure 32. Wrapping tinsel bodies.

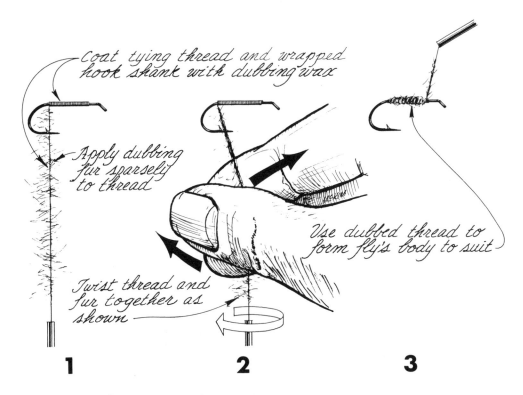

Coat tying thread and wrapped hook shank with dubbing wax

Apply dubbing fur sparsely to thread

Twist thread and fur together as shown

Use dubbed thread to form fly's body to suit

1   **2**   **3**

Figure 33. Single-stranded dubbing technique.

There are two techniques used to dub fur. Each has its good and bad points. The single-strand method shown in Figure 33 is a quick, versatile technique well suited to tying the bodies of smaller sized flies. It allows the tier to dub exactly the correct amount of tying thread with just the quantity of fur needed. The so-called "dubbing loop" method shown in Figure 34 can also be used to tie small flies, but it's especially well-suited to forming the heavier dubbed strands required for larger fly bodies where bulk is needed. Building large bodies by the single-strand technique is time consuming. The loop method, with its two-strand core is probably more durable as well, although this may not be of great import in very small flies.

The thing to remember when dubbing by the loop technique is the direction in which you twist the thread loop to form the dubbing strand. Imagine you are holding the thread at eye level and sighting down-thread toward the hook: if you're right-handed, you must twist the two strands together in the **counterclockwise** direction; if you're left-handed, twist the loop in the **clockwise** direction. The reason: forming the strand by twisting in the wrong direction will cause the loop to unwind as you wrap the body of the fly.

Both the single-strand and loop methods can be accomplished without the aid of tools; however, the simple dubbing tool shown in Appendix Plate 8 is a definite asset when dubbing by the loop technique. You can apply the dubbing fur or other material to be dubbed by adhering it loosely to the thread previously coated with wax or sticky cement. If you're using a loop, form what is called a "noodle." This is made by rolling the fur between the palms of your hands to compress it together, then shape it into a long, tapered form. The noodle is placed between the two strands of the thread loop and then twisted.

After the dubbed strand is formed, lift the strand and wrap it around the shank to make the fly's body. To create the shape desired, you can wrap it back and forth or in any way you choose until you're satisfied. Just be sure to finish wrapping at the point where it's to be tied off. Tie off the dubbed loop as you would any other strand-type body material and trim the excess. When using the single-strand method, remove the excess dubbing material from the thread and continue tying the fly.

12. Ribbing. The **rib** or **ribbing** on a fly is simply any material wrapped spirally over the

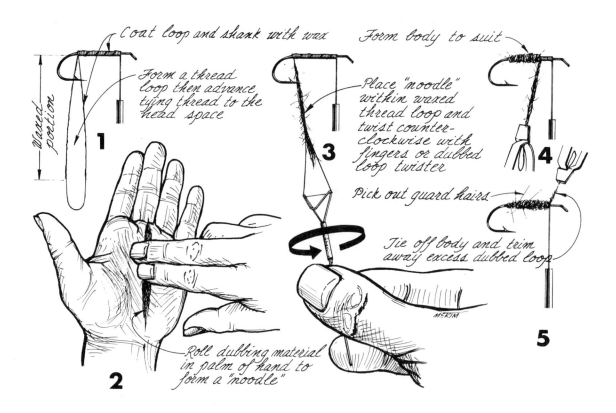

Coat loop and shank with wax

Form a thread loop then advance tying thread to the head space

Waxed position

1

Roll dubbing material in palm of hand to form a "noodle"

2

Form body to suit

Place "noodle" within waxed thread loop and twist counter-clockwise with fingers or dubbed loop twister

3

Pick out guard hairs

Tie off body and trim away excess dubbed loop

4

McKIM

5

Figure 34. Dubbing-loop technique.

body; that is, wrapped to reveal equal areas of body material between the wraps of ribbing material. Many types of materials may be used as ribbing — wire, tinsel, mylar, floss to name just a few. The idea is to simulate the segmented bodies of insects and crustaceans, such as shrimp, scud and other arthropods, or to add an extra measure of attraction to the fly. Ribbing also helps to strengthen the body construction.

Figure 35 illustrates the normal method used to rib the fly, usually in the same direction as thread is wrapped. But in flies with dubbed bodies the ribbing may proceed in the reverse rotation. Using this procedure helps to keep the rib from becoming lost to sight between the wraps of dubbed fur. Incidentally, this is one of the rare instances where the wrapping procedure is reversed in fly construction. It's a good idea to take one complete wrap of the rib around the shank before spiraling over the body itself. If you're ribbing a floss, mylar or other smooth body, you may also wish to apply a coat

of head cement before or after the rib is in place. When the rib has been applied to your satisfaction — and I suggest you examine the **back** side of the fly to make sure the wraps are equally spaced there as well — tie off as you would any body material and trim away the excess material.

13. Preparing and Applying Hackle-Type Feathers. Hackle and hackle type feathers, such as breast and flank feathers, are used in various ways to form parts of the fly. For example, barbs stripped from the quill may become the fly's tail and/or beard (legs), the entire feather may be palmered over the body or spun as the hackle, and the tips of the feather may be tied as wings, either horizontally or upright.

Although some patterns call for the feather to be tied in by its tip, the majority of flies having a palmered or spun hackle will specify that the feather be tied in near the butt of the quill. Before the feather is tied onto the hook, however, it must be prepared by removing the fluff (downy

58

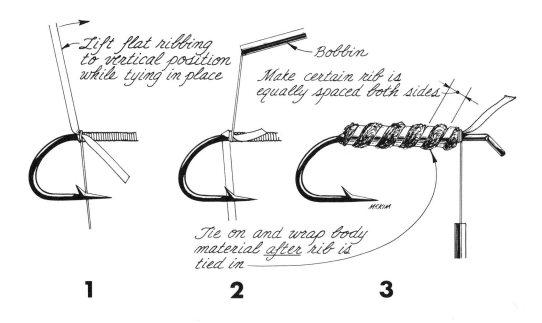

Figure 35. Applying the rib.

barbs near the butt) so that only the relatively stiff barbs become part of the fly. You can easily strip the fluff from a feather with your fingers, but this leaves a smooth quill that may subsequently pull loose during the palmering or spinning process. A much better way is to trim along each side of the quill with scissors as shown in Figure 36. This leaves a row of stubble barbs that help to anchor the quill in place and resist withdrawal when pressure is applied to wrap the feather tightly around the hook.

Trimming along the quill is a good general rule to adopt for preparing any feather used to form part of the fly. The "teeth" make it easier to

position feather wings and keeps them from rolling while you're tying them into place. The same is true for hackle tip wings. In both cases the stubble "teeth" makes the feather resist withdrawal.

Tie the feathers into place by the method shown in Figure 27 and trim off the excess butt, if any.

14. Palmered and Spun Hackles. The fact that the barbs of hackle-type feathers radiate outward when the feather is tightly wound around a hook shank is used to good advantage in tying flies. Feathers are wrapped in two ways: when the feather is wound in essentially the

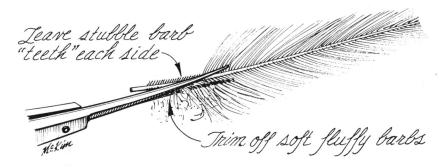

Figure 36. Preparing hackle type feathers.

59

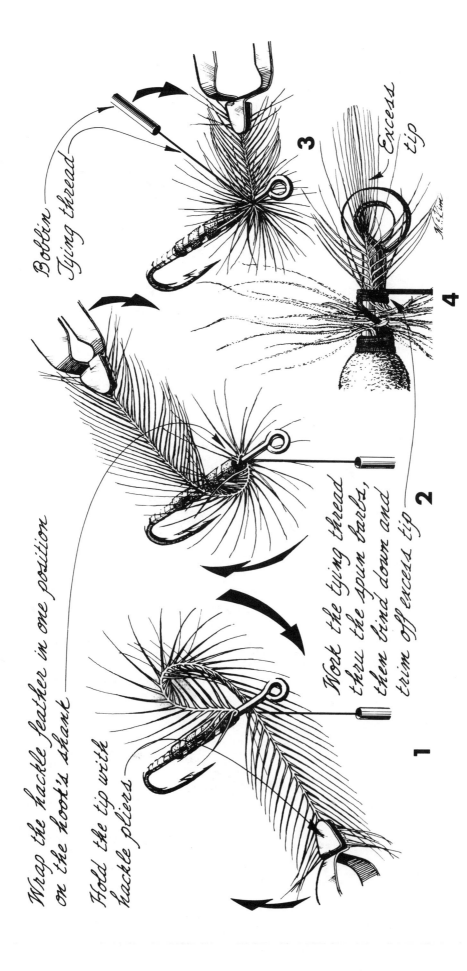

Wrap the hackle feather in one position on the hook's shank

Hold the tip with hackle pliers

Bobbin

Tying thread

Work the tying thread thru the spun barbs, then bind down and trim off excess tip

Excess tip

1

2

3

4

60

Figure 37. Spinning the hackle.

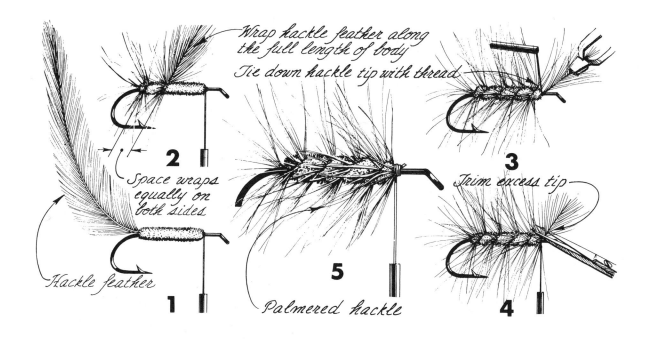

Figure 38. Palmering the hackle.

same location on the shank (Figure 37) then subsequently tied off so the barbs form a dense ring of radiating fibers, the hackle is called a **spun** hackle and the process is termed **spinning** the hackle; when it is tied in at one point on the shank and wound along its length to be tied off at another (Figure 38), the hackle is called a **palmered** hackle and the technique is termed **palmering.** The feather may be either a wet or dry fly type.

Although it is generally poor practice to trim spun hackle barbs (either before or after spinning), this is in fact one way of achieving the correct barb length when you're forced to use a feather too large for the fly being tied. Some tiers trim spun hackles as a matter of preference; others trim the spun barbs flat across the bottom to add stability and to help keep the fly from rolling on the water's surface. There may be times when you cannot avoid trimming. But if at all possible, I recommend you try to use a feather sized to the fly being tied. As a rule of thumb, for dry flies the length of spun hackle barbs should equal the distance from the head space to the point of the hook; in any case, not longer than from the head space to the tip of the hook's barb.

Palmered hackle, on the other hand, is very often trimmed in different ways to achieve special effects. Sometimes the barbs are all trimmed off close to the installed quill so that, in effect, the result is a fuzzy rib. The barbs on the top and sides of the palmered hackle may be trimmed off with scissors to leave the barbs under the body as the fly's legs. Or, the barbs on the rear of the body may be trimmed to leave a fuzzy rib while the front barbs may be trimmed in whole or part. There are hosts of possibilities for the imaginative fly tier.

After the feather is spun or palmered, it should be tied down as shown in Figure 30 and the excess tip of the feather removed. Here's where beginning tiers experience problems at first. If you are not careful with your scissors, you may trim away some of the barbs as well. Use the extreme tips of the scissors barely opened to locate and snip off the remaining quill. Better still, snap off the tip with a quick motion of your hand while holding the tip with hackle pliers. A little practice will make this an easy technique.

After you've secured the hackle into place, apply a drop of head cement on the point of connection. If the hackle is a spun type, apply

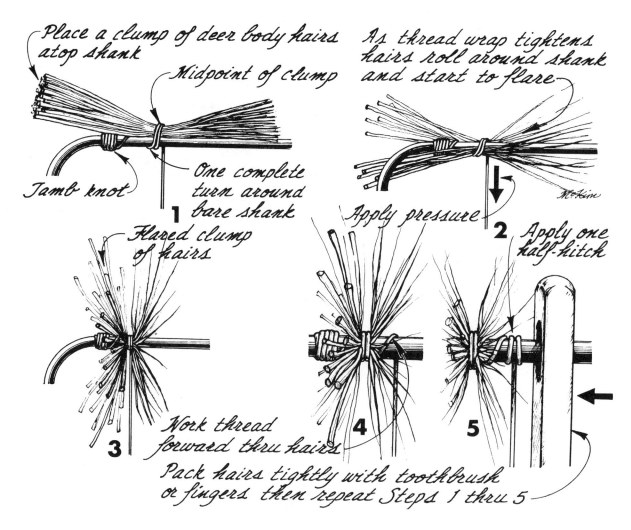

Place a clump of deer body hairs atop shank

Midpoint of clump

Jamb knot

One complete turn around bare shank

1

As thread wrap tightens hairs roll around shank and start to flare

Apply pressure

2

Apply one half-hitch

M°Kim

Flared clump of hairs

3

Work thread forward thru hairs

4

5

Pack hairs tightly with toothbrush or fingers then repeat Steps 1 thru 5

Figure 39. Spinning deer body hair.

thin head cement to the base of the barbs. Thinned cement has a tendency to be sucked into the clusters of barbs and acts to more firmly anchor the hackle in place.

15. Spun Deer Hair Bodies. Just as hackle feathers may be tied to radiate from the hook's shank, so can some hairs. The so-called "hollow" body hairs of members of the deer family can also be spun around a hook shank. As pointed out in Chapter Three, deer type hairs are not actually hollow. They are made of hollow air-filled cells that will compress when pinched. This single fact makes possible the tying of many hair bodied flies such as floating popping bugs and other patterns. Coupled with the tendency of the material, unless restrained, to roll around the shank as it's being tied into place, the compressibility of deer hair forms the basis for

the technique of spinning deer body hair illustrated in Figure 39 as follows:

To succeed at all you must spin deer hair around a bare shank. This reduces friction. Trim a clump of deer body hairs close to the cured hide of the animal and remove the fuzz with an old toothbrush. Hold the clump atop the bare shank and take two loose turns of tying thread around its middle. As you tighten the loops, relax your grip on the hairs. As the thread becomes tighter, the hairs will begin to bend in the middle and flare up from the hook while at the same time the moving thread will spread and roll them around the shank. When the thread wraps are tight, bring the thread forward by wrapping through the flared hairs and take two more wraps in front of the spun clump. With your fingernails next to the shank push the

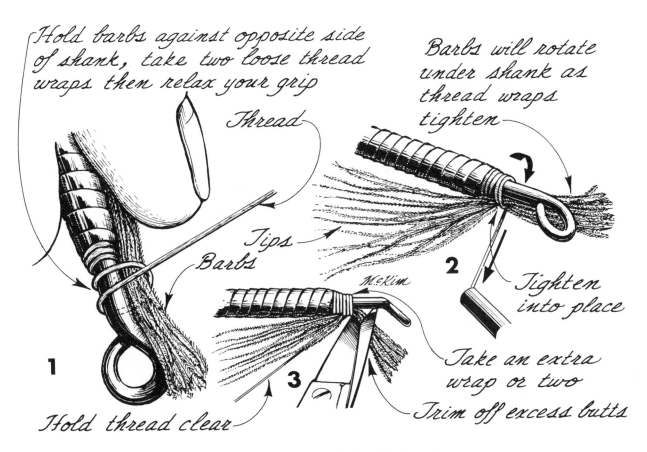

Figure 40. Tying the hackle beard.

flared clump back and tightly together, then repeat the procedure with more hair. One method many tiers use to jamb the spun hair into a dense mass is to run the eye and shank of the hook through the hole in the handle of a toothbrush, then use the hard plastic handle to apply more pressure. It's also a good idea to apply a half-hitch in front of each clump and to cement the connection with either head cement or a rubber type glue such as Glu-Bond. Another technique for spinning deer hair involves applying a half-hitch instead of two thread wraps over the middle of each clump, but the technique shown is fine for the beginner.

After the shank has been densely packed with spun hair and tied off, use your scissors or a razor blade to trim the body to the shape you want. Be careful not to trim off the other materials of which the fly is comprised, such as the legs and tail, if any.

16. Tying the Beard. The so-called **beard** on a fly is meant to simulate the swept back legs of an insect and to define the lower bodies of baitfish on streamer flies and bucktails. The correct positioning, tying in and, especially, the trimming off of excess beard materials usually presents some problems for the beginning fly tier. Holding the material in place under the shank is difficult to master at first, and trimming off the butts so close to the hanging tying thread frequently results in that most dreaded sound... the bobbin hitting the floor. More often than not, the previously tied in materials become loosened as the thread wraps unwind and the student groans in despair.

Perhaps I should make the point right here that when this happens all is not lost. Don't give up and feel you must start the fly all over again. Simply hold the fly's tied parts in place, grasp the end of the tying thread with the same hand and apply a jamb knot over the loosened wraps of thread. When the new jamb knot is secure, tighten the old wraps of thread by pulling on the loose end and trim off both free ends of tying thread. You may then proceed with the tying of the fly, having learned a valuable lesson.

There are two ways to tie in the beard. One way is to reverse the hook in the vise and tie the beard into place as shown in Figure 27. In this case, you're treating the beard material as you would any material tied atop the shank without running the risk of inadvertently cutting the tying thread in the process. A safe technique for the beginner.

However, it's not really necessary to turn the hook upside down to tie in the beard. Figure 40 shows another method that uses the rolling tendency of materials to good advantage. Simply swing the bobbin and thread away from the fly, place the clump of beard material against the far side of the fly and let the bobbin swing down. The weight of the bobbin will apply enough pressure to the thread to force the beard materials against the hook and hold them there. Now, take one wrap with the tying thread and tighten. As the thread constricts, it will transport the beard to its proper position under the hook. Check the beard for length and shorten or lengthen it as necessary. Hold the beard in place, apply several more wraps of thread and trim the excess. Be very careful not to cut the tying thread in the process.

17. Tying the Wing. Although there are many styles of fly wings, made from a wide variety of materials, only a few types — fortunately — present difficulty to the beginning fly tier. Fly wings derive their characteristic appearances (see Appendix Plate 4, Fly Wing Types) from the kinds of materials of which they're made and the thread wrapping techniques used *after* the wing or wings are secured on to the hook. Most wings are initially tied in place by the technique shown in Figure 27. Their final positions are maintained by several other techniques I'll describe shortly.

In brief, the most common problems beginners have with wings are as follows: The wing, or one of a pair of wings, is either; 1) too long or too short; 2) has rolled around the shank and the fly

is no longer symmetrical; 3) is cocked at the wrong angle or, in the case of quill segment wings; 4) one side is concave while the other is convex, and/or 5) the barbs have split apart into a ragged rumble. Most of these problems have simple solutions and all of them smooth out and disappear with enough practice. It's well to have an understanding of why they become a problem in the first place because then you'll know what to look out for. I also have a few suggestions to offer that should help you avoid most problems and make the task of tying the more difficult wings easier. So let's examine each problem in turn.

First, the type of wing usually dictates the lengthwise orientation of the material as it's tied on top of the hook. For example, a downwing will normally be tied with the **butts** toward the eye; an upwing with the **tips** toward the eye. To be certain the wing will be the correct length, hold the wing material against the fly in its proper orientation and position, select the point of connection and form the twin loops shown in Figure 27 **exactly** where you intend to tie it down. Before the loops are finally tightened, however, check the length to be sure and, if necessary, adjust the wing forward or backward. Cinch the thread tight. To prevent the wing from rolling around the shank, hold the wing firmly as you secure it in place. While there are specific exceptions to the rule, after the wing is cinched down you should trim the excess material off at a shallow angle and wrap down the remaining butts with tying thread. This makes a smoothly tapered transition to the next material.

One of the most important things to remember when tying the wing is to properly prepare the wing material. Always trim off the barbs as shown in Figure 36 when the whole feather or its tip is used to form the wing. Clean the fuzz from the butts of bucktail and other hair wing materials before tying them into place. Tie in only the amount of material the pattern calls for, no more, no less. I'll describe the special preparation of so-called "quill" wings later in

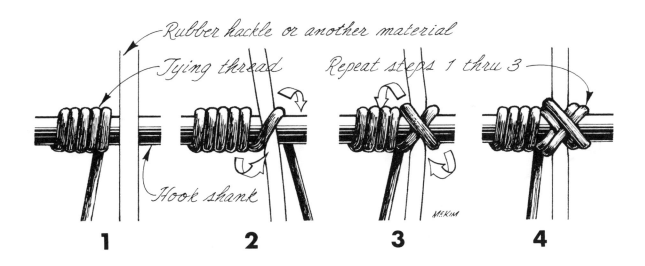

Figure 41. The "figure '8'" wrap.

this discussion.

Wings vary widely in slhouette. They may be tied singly or in pairs, and even paired wings may be tied to appear as a single entity or be divided in varying degree. A few are meant to be tied flatly parallel to the shank along the sides or on top of the body but most wings rise from the body at an angle, often with their tips splayed apart. Some wings are a solitary vertical shaft, others are divided to form a "vee" when viewed from in front of the fly. Spent wings are tied perpendicular to the shank, appearing as a straight line when seen from the front. Depending upon the natural curvature of the feathers, some wings fan apart to present yet another silhouette. The simple wrapping techniques used to achieve these differing configurations are applied after the wing material is already secured in place. One consists of the standard thread wrapping technique shown in Figure 25; the others are techniques shown in Figure 41 and Figure 42.

To clarify the use of these techniques, let's take the following examples: if the wing is to be a hair downwing that slants upward and back from the eye, lift the wing material and apply thread wraps behind and close to its base until it assumes the correct angle. If the wing is an upright wing, lift the material and apply sufficient thread wraps to the front (and back, if

required) of the wing to anchor it in the vertical position. In fact, the examples illustrated in Figure 42 are typical of the procedures used to position most wings. In the case of hackled dry flies, additional wing reinforcement is provided when the hackle is spun in front and back of the wing, while in parachute hackled flies the hackle and wing reinforce each other. A drop of head cement at the base of the wing should become standard practice.

To maintain the correct angle between paired wings, use the "figure 8" wrapping technique shown in Figure 41. The "figure 8" allows you not only to divide the wings until they assume the proper angle, or "vee," but to station each wing of the pair symmetrically with respect to the body of the fly. It's also an excellent way to splay the tails of a fly, secure the legs of popping bugs and shape other parts of the fly.

The most difficult type of wing to master is without doubt the so-called "quill wing." Not only are many tempers lost while learning to tie quill wings, but even the name is misleading. Quill wings are not made from the quill of the feather; rather, the name derives from the fact that the wing material consists of sections (or segments) of "zippered" barbs trimmed from the vane-like surfaces of primary or secondary wing (often called "quill") feathers of waterfowl. The naturally curved shape and texture of such

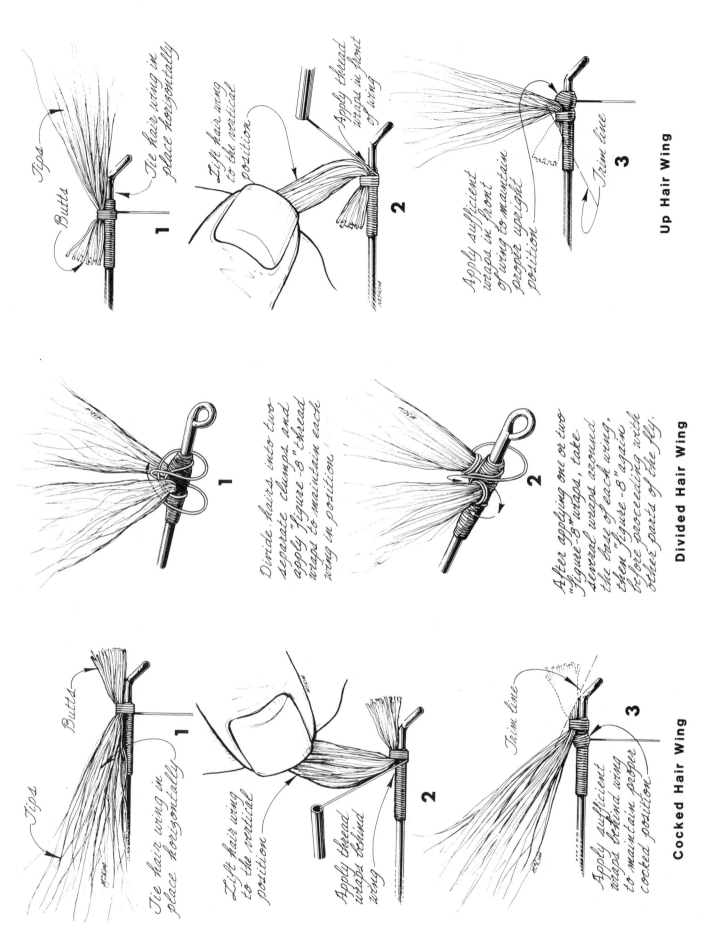

Up Hair Wing

1. Tie hair wing in place horizontally
   Tips
   Butts

2. Lift hair wing to the vertical position
   Apply thread wraps in front of wing

3. Apply sufficient wraps in front of wing to maintain proper upright position
   Trim line

Divided Hair Wing

1. Divide hairs into two separate clumps and apply "figure-8" thread wraps to maintain each wing in position

2. After applying one or two "figure-8" wraps, take several wraps around the base of each wing, then "figure-8" again before proceeding with other parts of the fly.

Cocked Hair Wing

1. Tie hair wing in place horizontally
   Butts
   Tips

2. Lift hair wing to the vertical position
   Apply thread wraps behind wing

3. Trim line
   Apply sufficient wraps behind wing to maintain proper cocked position

Figure 42. Positioning hair wings.

66

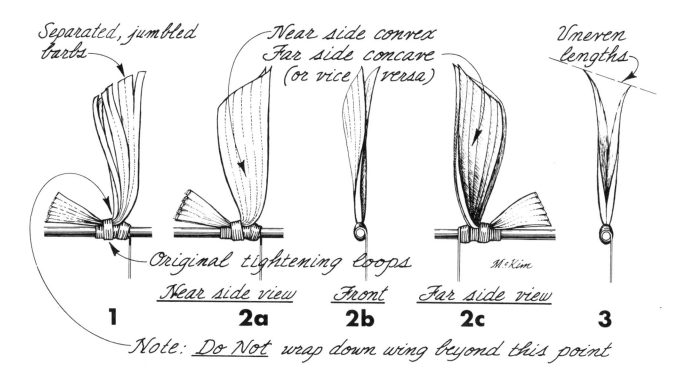

Separated, jumbled barbs

Near side convex
Far side concave
(or vice versa)

Uneven lengths

Original tightening loops

Near side view

Front

Far side view

McKim

1   2a   2b   2c   3

Note: *Do Not* wrap down wing beyond this point

Figure 43. Defective quill wings.

sections have long been appreciated by fly tiers. Correctly tied, they're among the most beautifully natural looking of dry fly wings.

Then why are they so difficult to tie? For one thing, to tie quill sections into place so that all of the fibers are compressed together in a straight line requires you to perfectly execute the technique shown in Figure 27. If not, one side — usually the side away from the tier — will be concave, while the near side will be flat or convex. Both sides should look identical. For another, quill sections tend to separate into individual barbs when: 1) they are roughly handled; 2) additional thread wraps are placed on the wing in **front** of its original point of connection to the hook; or 3) the fly's hackle is carelessly spun. Figure 43 illustrates these defects.

How can you avoid these problems? Practice...and lots of it. I also suggest you try the following: select right and left primary feathers that closely match in size and shape. Apply a light coat of women's hair spray or any brand of clear fixative spray to the feathers' shiny

undersides and let dry thoroughly. This will help to bind the barbs and keep the cutaway sections intact. Use the gap of a hook of the same size as the one upon which you've tied the fly (as shown in Figure 44) to measure the width of the wing section and separate it from the other barbs. Trim out matching sections from each feather close to the quill. Place both sections in the palm of one hand, moisten the tip of your free forefinger and use it to pick up one section. Place it on top of the other section. Both tips should be even. Now, pick up the two sections together by their tips, position them atop the hook with the tips toward the eye, transfer your grip to the opposite hand and tie the wing sections into place by the method shown in Figure 27. You will find that the correct positioning of your thumb and forefinger is the crucial and determining factor as to whether the wing will be straight or concave. This can only be learned through trial and error.

Thanks to Bill Charles, an innovative fly tier from Chicago, I can offer you an easy way out, a method whereby you will be able to tie perfect

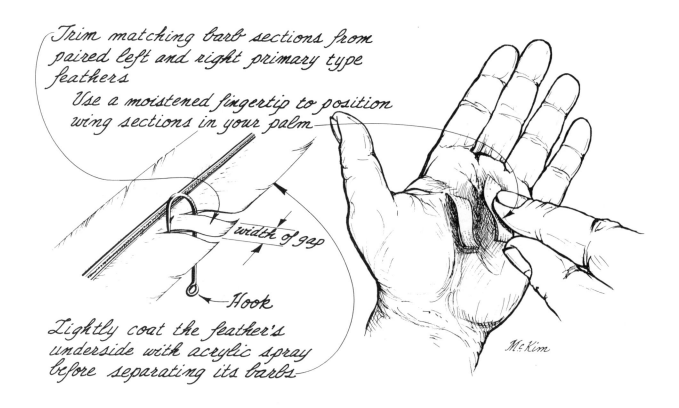

Trim matching barb sections from paired left and right primary type feathers

Use a moistened fingertip to position wing sections in your palm

width of gap

Hook

Lightly coat the feather's underside with acrylic spray before separating its barbs

McKim

Figure 44. Measuring quill wing sections.

quill wings every time. All you need is some type of level jawed clamping device. A spring type clothespin, an ACCO clamp or even a small bench vise will do. After you've paired up the quill sections and measured the correct length of the wing, place the butt ends together in the clamp as shown in Figure 45. Make certain the exposed parts are the correct length of the fly's wing. Wax a length of **silk** tying thread and form the type of loop shown. Place the loop over the wing tips and draw it tight, being careful to keep the tightening loop next to the clamp. When the loop is cinched tight, apply a drop of head cement to the connection and let it dry. You will find when the wing is removed from the clamp that all of the barbs have been compressed in a perfectly straight line and the wing is symmetrical and perfectly formed, ready to tie atop the hook. It's then a simple matter to tie it in place, lift it to the proper orientation and apply the necessary wraps of thread to keep it there.

Before I leave the subject of tying fly wings, there's yet another technique that will make it easier for you to secure hair downwings such as bucktail atop the shank so that all of the hairs remain in one place, tightly compressed together. The method is shown in Figure 46. Firmly hold the clump of hairs atop the shank as you tighten the vertical "figure 8" wrap, then apply several more standard wraps of thread to finish tying the wing into place.

18. Forming the Head. Here's the point at which loud groans of frustration and sighs of dismay are normally heard throughout a group of beginners. After much fumbling, wrapping, unwrapping and rewrapping, finally the tail, body, wing and other parts of the fly have been applied and the fly is almost complete. But, what happened to the space where the head needs to be? Well, little by little it became crowded with encroaching materials until little if any space remained. Maybe that's a good thing. It drives

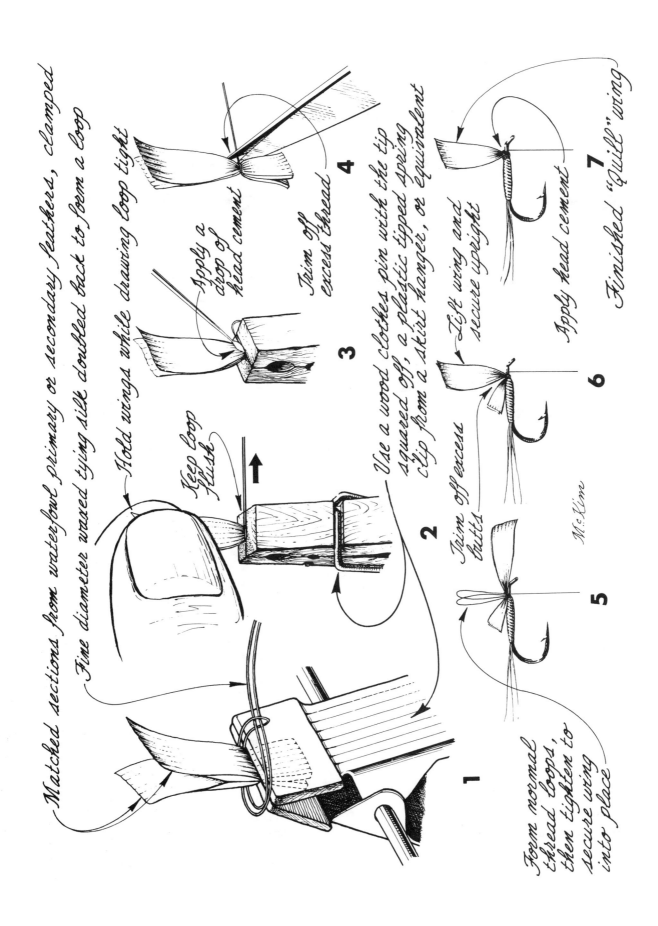

Matched sections from waterfowl primary or secondary feathers, clamped

Fine diameter waxed tying silk doubled back to form a loop

Hold wings while drawing loop tight

Keep loop flush

Form normal thread loops, then tighten to secure wing into place

1

2

Use a wood clothes pin with the tip squared off, a plastic tipped spring clip from a skirt hanger, or equivalent

Apply a drop of head cement

3

Trim off excess thread

4

Trim off excess butts

5

McKim

Lift wing and secure upright

6

Apply head cement

Finished "quill" wing

7

Figure 45. Bill Charles' quill wing tying technique.

69

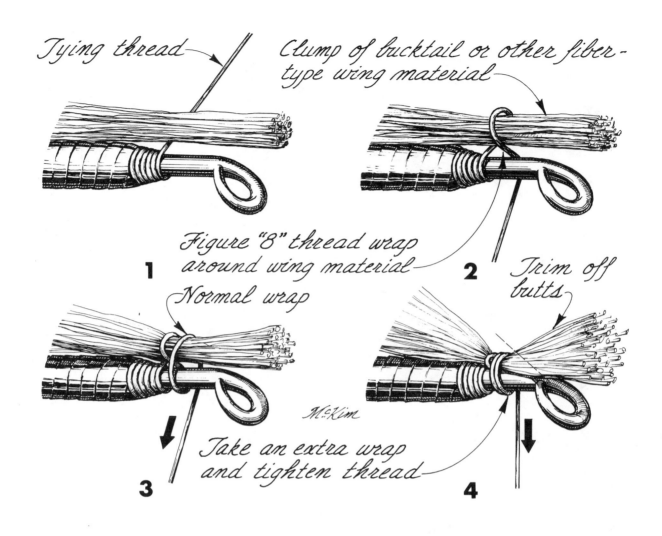

Tying thread

Clump of bucktail or other fiber-type wing material

1

Figure "8" thread wrap around wing material

Normal wrap

2

Trim off butts

3

Take an extra wrap and tighten thread

McKim

4

Figure 46. Hair downwing tying technique.

home the point I made at the beginning of this chapter — **don't crowd the head space**!

Let's assume you've remembered, or are one of the lucky ones, and you're ready to form the head. Simply apply consecutive even wraps of tying thread to build it up to the shape and size called for by the pattern of fly you're tying. Avoid lapping the wraps over each other; this will result in unsightly lumps. To form an oval head that's evenly tapered from each end, stop the wraps one turn short of each end on succeeding layers of thread and the head will thicken in the center Stopping short on one end only will cause the head to taper in that one direction. One of the instructional fly patterns in

the next chapter — the "ANT" — is designed to teach the type of thread control required to form perfectly proportioned heads and other thread wrapped parts of flies.

After you have built the head to the proper shape and proportion **unwrap** 3 to 5 turns of thread and whip finish the same number of wraps carefully back into place. Complete the knot and you're almost finished with the fly. There is, however, one important exception to the standard procedure just described: if the fly is a dry fly, eliminate all unnecessary weight. The head on a dry fly should normally be as small as possible, so form the head with the whip finish only. Three to five turns are ample.

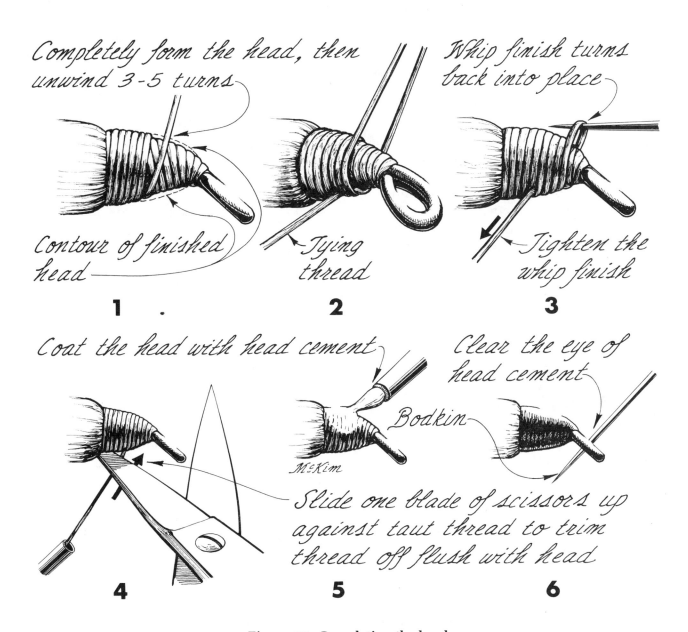

Figure 47. Completing the head.

When you've finished tying off the head, use your fly tying scissors to trim away the tying thread as shown in Figure 47. **Do not cut** the thread by squeezing the handles as you would normally cut material. This will inevitably leave a short stub of thread under the head of the fly. Instead, hold the thread taut with one hand while you slide one blade of the scissors up against the thread to the head. A slight sawing movement will neatly sever the thread flush with the underside of the head, leaving no visible evidence to mark the spot.

19. Coating the Head and Completing the Fly.
After the head is completed and the tying thread has been trimmed off, you must coat the head with head cement or another material such as epoxy. This lends the fly a finished look and, more importantly, prevents the whip finish knot from loosening during use. To allow the cement to flow evenly over the entire head it should be kept thinned to a flowable consistency; in fact, thinned head cement offers another advantage when it's applied to the heads of spun hackled patterns. The cement seeps into and around the

base of the barbs and effectively binds the entire hackle into place.

But head cement, especially very thin head cement, also has a nasty tendency to flow in the wrong direction — right into the eye of the fly hook. There it clogs the eye solidly, a condition that becomes maddeningly apparent while you're trying to change flies standing waist deep in an icy stream in fading light...with trout rising everywhere! When this happens, for want of a needle you can use the point of another small fly's hook to clear the eye. Better still, you can avoid the problem altogether by just developing the habit of clearing the eyes of all flies as you finish tying them. After you've coated the head, insert the point of your dubbing needle into the eye as shown in Figure 47. Leave the point in place until the head cement has hardened. This is important. Often the cement simply flows together again as soon as the needle's point is withdrawn, leaving the eye as clogged as before.

When your fly is finished, take a moment to spruce it up before placing it in your fly box. Use the bodkin to straighten out the spun hackle or to pick out the guard hairs on dubbed bodies to give them the shaggy look fish adore. Straighten the wings and, if necessary, recock them to the proper angle. If your fly is a hair bug, you will need to give it a precise haircut. Or retouch the paint on a cork bodied pattern. Soak or spray your dry flies in Scotch-Gard water repellent. Only after you're satisfied you've done the best job of which you're capable should you consider the fly complete. Truly dedicated fly tiers tie flies to satisfy themselves first, the fish second.

Conclusion. You're now as ready as you need to be to tackle the patterns in the next and final chapter of this book. If you get into trouble along the line, you can always refer back to this and other chapters and to the *Glossary of Fly Tying Terms* when you're confused. The *Appendix* and suggested reading found in the section titled *Sources* should provide other information of value.

If there's one word of wisdom I have to offer, it's this: The perfect fly for the ultimate fish is still a figment of someone's imagination.... maybe yours. So let your ideas roam wild and free. Try anything, tie everything. Use different colors, materials, sizes. Imitate the bugs you see.... and some that could never be. Just be sure to let Mr. Trout or Mrs. Bass be the final judges. Gosh, if one six-pound bonito shockingly lacked the good sense to reject my own improbable creation, why not offer one of yours?

I'll leave you now to try your wings... and bodies and tails... in the sincere hope you too may share my obsession with fur, feathers and fun.

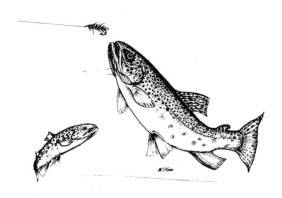

V

The Flies

In this chapter you will tie a number of differing patterns. All share one thing in common: each fly can be counted upon to take the kind of fish with which it has become identified, not necessarily the species for which it was designed.

You might ask "Why?", and if you mean "Why does it produce?", only the fish know the truth of that. But if you mean "Why is that fly **tied** that way?", the answer is simple: its originator believed his choice of materials and silhouette might just prove irresistible. If the pattern evolved from the observed tastes and behavior of the species for which it was designed, I prefer to conclude this to be manifest proof of the originator's acumen and vision. On the other hand, it could just as easily have been the result of happy coincidence. No fly tier can ever be sure beforehand his creation will prove successful. Fish comprise the supreme court of angling.

Because I believe the "why" and "where" will serve to increase the fun of tying, I've included wherever known a little background on each pattern, plus a few thoughts along the way on various fly types and their applications.

Panfish Patterns

When it comes to panfish, I like to paraphrase the late Will Rogers: "I never met a bluegill I didn't like." And I'm not alone. Millions of anglers are fans of these scrappy little fighters and their relatives, all members of the North American sunfish family of which Mr. Bass is king. Who could dislike a fish that's found nearly everywhere in huge abundance, that when hooked battles out of all proportion to its size, takes a fly as readily as a worm and is mighty good eatin' to boot?

During that special paradise called spawning season, bluegills will gobble dry flies, wet flies, tiny cork bugs — even bass poppers nearly their own size. Indeed, flies in endless variety will produce bluegill strikes and often the simplest patterns are the best. That's one of the main reasons we've chosen to begin with two very effective but easy to tie patterns — Dave Johnson's "**Just A Bug**" (Pattern No. 1) and Dan Gapen's "**Timber Wolf**" (Pattern No. 2). We suggest you tie each in the size or sizes specified and vary the colors of the materials. Often a different color or combination of colors, as well as a change in the size of the fly, will make the difference between acceptance or rejection in a given situation.

Pattern No. 1 — **Just a Bug**
Tied by Dave Johnson

Pattern No. 2 — **Timber Wolf**
Tied by Dave Johnson

Pattern No. 3 — **Ant**
Tied by John McKim

Pattern No. 4 — **Skunk Woolly Worm**
Tied by Larry B. Stoner

Pattern No. 5 — **Yuk Bug**
Tier unknown

Pattern No. 6 — **Lowe's Grey Nymph**
Tied by John McKim

Pattern No. 7 — **Cross Fox Nymph**
Tied by W.D. Hess

Pattern No. 8 — **Warden's Worry**
Tied by Harris E. Streety

Pattern No. 9 — **Brindle Bug**
Tied by John McKim

Pattern No. 10 — **Anonymous Peacock**
Tied by Dan Sundberg

Pattern No. 11 — **Black Nosed Dace**
Tied by John McKim

Pattern No. 12 — **Hornberg**
Tied by John McKim

Pattern No. 13 — **Snake Fly**
Tied by John McKim

Pattern No. 14 — **Sand Crab**
Tied by Ned Grey

Pattern No. 15 — **Cheater Adams**
Tied by John McKim

Pattern No. 16 — **Kings River Caddis**
Tied by John McKim

Pattern No. 17 — **McKim's Evadry**
Tied by John McKim

Pattern No. 18 — **Humpy**
Tied by Clarence Tarbet

Pattern No. 19 — **Poly Mayfly**
Tied by Grant Mounteer

Pattern No. 20 — **McKim's Weatherbug**
Tied by John McKim

Pattern No. 21 — **Stoner's Bass Bug**
Tied by Larry B. Stoner

Pattern No. 22 — **Salmon Black**
Tied by Edward L. Haas

Pattern No. 23 — **Gilled Caddis Larva**
Tied by Wayne Luallen

Pattern No. 24 — **McKim's Evafloat'n Frog**
Tied by John McKim

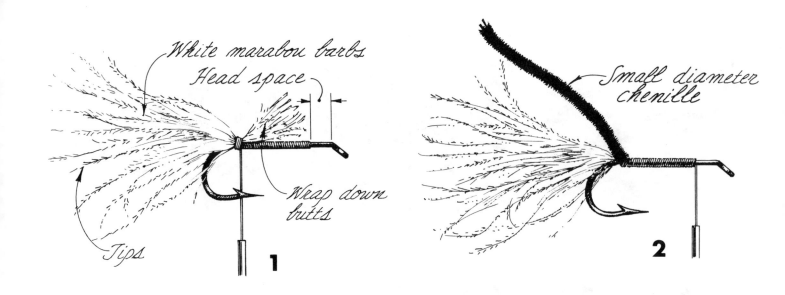

White marabou barbs

Head space

Wrap down butts

Tips

1

Small diameter chenille

2

PATTERN NO. 1

Just A Bug

Type: Wet Fly

Simulates: Small minnow or insect

Habitat: Lakes, ponds, streams

Takes: Bluegills and other panfish

Background: This fly was originated by Dave Johnson, Knightstown, Indiana specifically for bluegills. Very effective.

Materials:
    Hook: Sizes 12, 10, 8 Mustad #3906 TDE Bronzed
    Thread: Size "A" Nylon, White
    Tail: White Marabou Barbs
    Body: Black or Orange Chenille, Small Diameter
    Head: Tying Thread

1. Leave head space. Wrap the tying thread to the hook's bend and tie in a clump of marabou barbs to form a tail 1½ times shank length.

2. Tie in 2-3 inches of chenille then wrap the tying thread back to the head space.

3. Coat the thread covered shank with head cement. While wet, form a closely wrapped chenille body and tie off at the head space. Trim off excess chenille.

4. Form a relatively large head and whip finish. Clip tying thread and apply head cement. Be sure to clear the eye of hardened cement.

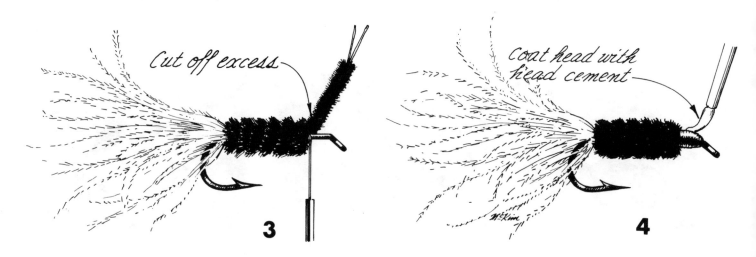

Cut off excess

3

Coat head with head cement

4

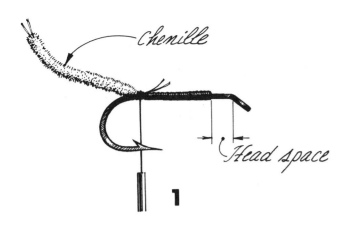

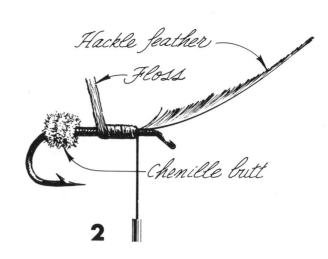

PATTERN 2

Timber Wolf

Type: Wet Fly

Simulates: Insect

Habitat: Freshwater lakes, ponds, streams

Takes: Trout, panfish

Background: This fly was originated by Dan Gapen, Big Lake, Minnesota, for trout in the Yellowstone area. Very effective bluegill fly as well.

Materials:

Hook: Size 12, 10, 8 Mustad #3906 TDE, Bronzed
Thread: Size "A" Nylon, White or Black
Butt: Yellow Chenille, Small Diameter
Hackle: Badger or Brown
Body: Brown or White Floss
Head: Tying Thread

1. Leave head space. Closely wrap the tying thread to the hook's bend. Tie in 1-2 inches of chenille.

2. Form a chenille butt of three wraps close together, tie off and trim the excess chenille. Wrap tying thread forward. Near the head space tie in the hackle feather, concave side up, tip forward. Tie in 3-4 inches of floss. Apply thinned head cement over the thread base and wrap the floss evenly back to the butt.

3. Reverse and wrap forward, covering the first layer of floss. Tie off with several binding wraps of thread and trim the excess floss.

4. Spin the hackle, leaving some of the tip to form a single wing. Tie the hackle and wing down to sweep toward the rear. Form a rounded thread head and whip finish. Clip the thread and apply head cement. Be sure to clear the eye of hardened cement.

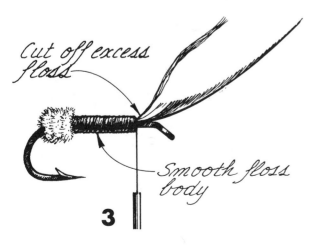

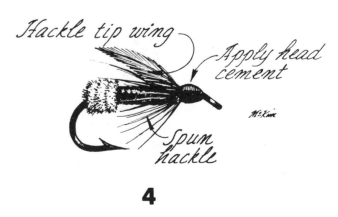

Black Flying Ant

Kings Caterpillar

Dave's Paper Wing Hopper

British Beetle

Terrestrials...
Chance Delicacies

The main diet of wild trout consists of various aquatic insects such as Mayflies, Stoneflies and Caddisflies, freshwater crustaceans such as scuds (Amphipods) and shrimp (Decapods), and swimming molluscs (Pteropods) and any fish small enough to eat, including their own kind. While trout can be exasperatingly selective, they will, on occasion, accept more exotic fare — worms, garlic flavored cheese, marshmallows and artificial flies.

All sorts of fly patterns, many of a design resembling nothing in nature, have taken trout. Still, it's always a safer bet to offer something that's at least vaguely similar to the food the fish is used to seeing. That includes "terrestrials," those otherwise inaccessible land dwellers that fate frequently places within reach. When rain washes the land and streams erode their banks an almost infinite variety of living forms become fair game. At such times a caterpillar, a grasshopper or an ant pattern can be deadly.

Several of the instructional patterns included in this book were derived from terrestrial insects. Those resembling caterpillars simulate pre-adult forms of the species. Flies patterned after winged adults, such as moths (not illustrated herein) can be very effective at times. The simple "Ant" (Pattern No. 3), an adult

imitation, has been included for yet another reason: to tie the "Ant" properly requires precise thread control, a technique that will serve you well in the construction of all flies. The most important thing to remember in tying the "Ant" is to keep your thread short (bobbin to fly) at all times, and to avoid the hook's sharp point. One nick and you may be forced to start all over.

PATTERN NO. 3

Ant

Type: Wet Fly, Terrestrial

Simulates: Land dwelling insect

Habitat: Freshwater lakes, ponds, streams

Takes: Trout and panfish

Background: Origins unknown

Materials:
  Hook: Sizes 8-16 Mustad #3906 TDE Bronzed
  Thread: Flat Strand Nylon, Black or Red
  Abdomen: Tying Thread
  Legs: Brown Neck Hackle, Dry Quality
  Thorax: Tying Thread
  Head: Tying Thread

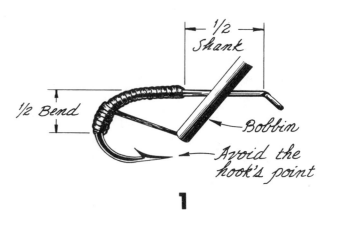

1. Start the fly at mid-shank. Wrap solidly to mid-bend, then reverse direction and wrap evenly forward over the thread base. Stop one wrap short of where you began the fly.

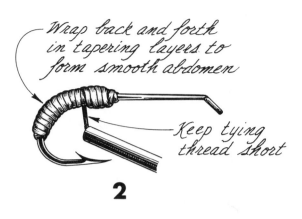

Wrap back and forth in tapering layers to form smooth abdomen

Keep tying thread short

2

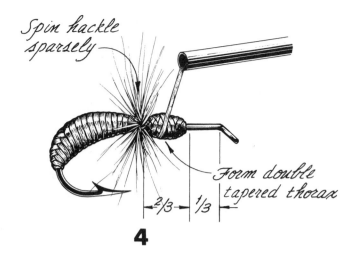

Spin hackle sparsely

Form double tapered thorax

2/3 ~ 1/3

4

2. Again reverse direction and wrap toward the bend. Stop one wrap short of the last underlying wrap and again reverse direction. Continue this wrapping procedure until you have formed a smoothly double-tapered abdomen and the tying thread is again suspended at mid-shank. Coat the finished abdomen with head cement and let thoroughly dry.

3. Tie in the hackle feather with its concave side up, tip extending toward the bend. The barb length should equal the hook's gap. Trim off the excess butt.

4. Spin the hackle at mid-shank 2-3 turns, tie off and trim the excess tip. The hackle should appear as rather sparse legs. Now form the fly's thorax using the same technique used for the abdomen.

5. Form a head about one-half the diameter of the thorax and whip finish. Clip the tying thread and coat both the head and thorax with head cement. Be sure to clear the eye of hardened cement.

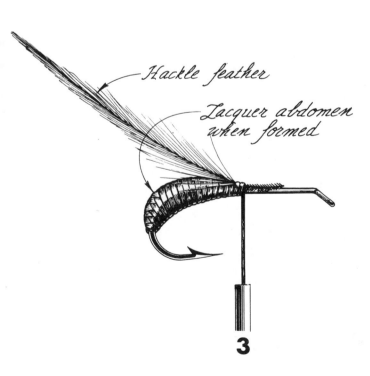

Hackle feather

Lacquer abdomen when formed

3

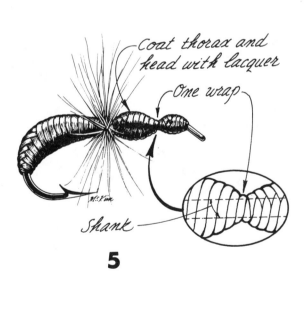

Coat thorax and head with lacquer

One wrap

Shank

5

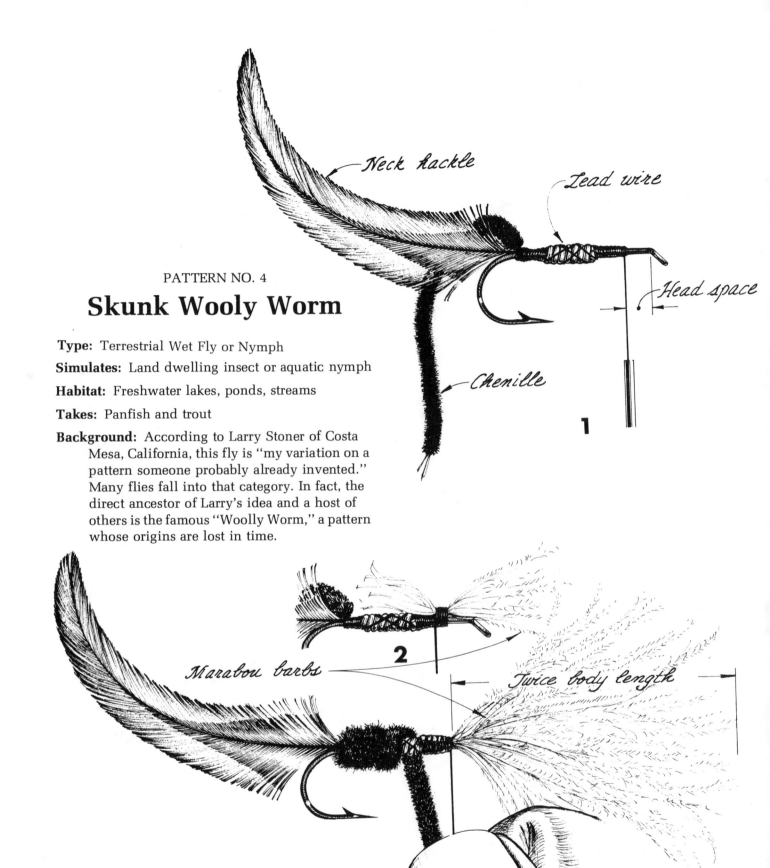

PATTERN NO. 4

Skunk Wooly Worm

Type: Terrestrial Wet Fly or Nymph

Simulates: Land dwelling insect or aquatic nymph

Habitat: Freshwater lakes, ponds, streams

Takes: Panfish and trout

Background: According to Larry Stoner of Costa Mesa, California, this fly is "my variation on a pattern someone probably already invented." Many flies fall into that category. In fact, the direct ancestor of Larry's idea and a host of others is the famous "Woolly Worm," a pattern whose origins are lost in time.

Neck hackle

Lead wire

Head space

Chenille

1

Marabou barbs

2

Twice body length

3

80

Materials:

    Hook: Sizes 14-10 Std to 2XL, Mustad #3906 TDE
        Bronzed

    Thread: Size 6/0 Prewaxed or larger, depending
        upon the hook

    Hackle: Black or Dark Brown Neck Hackle, Wet,
        Palmered

    Underbody: Small Diameter Black Chenille over
        4-6 Wraps of 0.18 Diam. Lead Wire

    Overbody and Tail: White Marabou Barbs

    Head: Tying Thread

1. Leave ample head space. Wrap to the hook's bend and tie in the hackle feather. Tie in 2-3 inches of chenille. Weight the mid-shank with 4-6 turns of lead wire and secure into place with tying thread.

2. Wrap to the head space and tie in a clump of marabou barbs with the tips extending approximately 2 body lengths beyond the eye.

3. Coat the weighted shank with head cement and closely wrap the chenille forward to the head space. Tie off and trim away the excess chenille.

4. Now bring the marabou barbs backward atop the chenille body, hold them tautly and "rib" (spiral wrap) the barbs into place with tying thread.

5. Secure the base of the tail firmly, then "rib" the thread forward to the head space, taking care to evenly cross-hatch opposing thread ribs.

6. Palmer the hackle feather forward directly above the thread rib and tie it down at the head space.

7. Trim off the hackle's tip and form a good sized head. Whip finish and clip the thread. Coat the head with head cement.

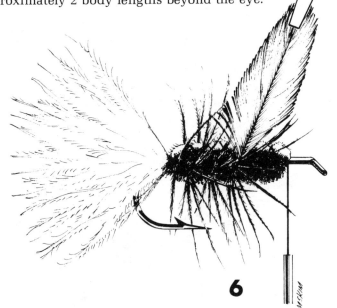

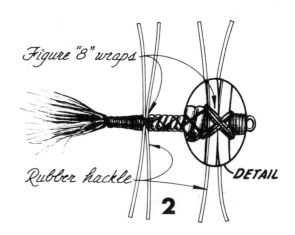

Squirrel tail

Lead wire

1

Figure "8" wraps

Rubber hackle

DETAIL

2

PATTERN NO. 5

Yuk Bug

Type: Wet Fly, Terrestrial

Simulates: Land dwelling insect

Habitat: Freshwater lakes, ponds, streams

Takes: Trout and panfish

Background: No one has been able to pin down who actually originated this fly, a sort of "Woolly Worm/Girdle Bug" hybrid. According to John Spencer, proprietor of the Four Rivers Sport Shop in Twin Bridges, Montana, someone in his area developed the fly and it has since become a standard on the Big Hole, Beaverhead and Jefferson Rivers. And...let's face it, it's a downright ugly fly, but who said trout hate ugly flies. Fact is, lunker browns love it, and if esthetics were the major criteria for deceiving fish who could begin to estimate the number of patterns to disqualify? The "Yuk Bug" is rugged, so don't fret to keep it pretty for fish presentation. And tie it BIG, nothing less than sizes 2, 4 or 6.

Materials:

Hook: Sizes 2, 4, 6 Mustad #38941 or #9672 TDE Bronzed

Thread: Size "A" Nylon

Tail: Grey Squirrel Tail
Weight: Medium Lead Wire
Legs: Small Rubber Hackle
Hackle: Badger or Grizzly; Palmered; Wet Quality
Body: Black Chenille; Large Diameter
Head: Tying Thread

1. Leave ample head space. Wrap shank to bend and tie in tail. Weight shank with lead wraps and secure into place.

2. Tie two pairs of rubber hackle legs atop the shank, one pair behind the head space, the second pair just forward of the hook's point. Figure "8" wrap into place. Trim legs to desired length, equally both sides. Return thread to the tail.

3. Tie in the hackle feather securely at the tail, its tip toward the rear. Strip the end of a length of chenille, tie down the core strands at the tail, double the strands back and tie down securely.

4. Coat the lead-wrapped shank with head cement. While still wet, wrap the chenille body, tie off and trim off the excess chenille. Palmer the hackle forward, tie down at the head space and trim off the excess tip. Form a relatively small head and whip finish. Clip the thread and coat the head with head cement. Clear the eye.

Badger or Grizzly hackle

Black chenille

3

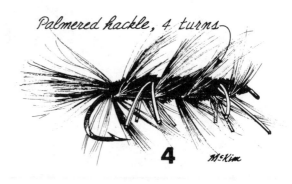

Palmered hackle, 4 turns

4

McKim

Nymph?
Or Wet Fly?

Sometimes it's easy to confuse the two. Indeed, even experts may on occasion disagree as to whether a certain fly is a wet fly or a nymph. Both types, as a matter of simple fact, are "wet" type flies intended to be fished entirely submerged. But then, so are streamers, bucktails and many terrestrial patterns.

As a type, the classic wet fly traditionally implied a down-wing sinking pattern tied to simulate a drowned flying insect, or perhaps a live one trapped by the water's surface tension and sucked by turbulence under the surface. The wet fly was originally limited to freshwater applications. Today, with the emergence of saltwater fly fishing, many "wet fly" silhouettes have proved effective for saltwater species.

Conversely, nymphs — at least in theory — simulate the immature (or pre-emergent) stages in the lives of certain genera of freshwater aquatic insects such as Mayflies and Stoneflies. These are the forms in which these insects spend 99 percent of their lives. In fly tying practice, however, the term "nymph" is often misapplied to other aquatic forms such as Caddisfly larva and scud.

From an academic standpoint — particularly among fly tying purists — the distinction between wet flies and nymphs may be worthy of argument. But if your interest lies in the direction of applied fly tying, just remember: while trout (and other gamefish) are frequently exposed to the sight of drowned winged insects, they're continuously exposed to nymph-like forms. Nymphs and nymph-like creatures comprise the bulk of a trout's diet. So, when you present a fair facsimile of something a fish is most used to seeing the odds are vastly greater that your product will tempt a strike.

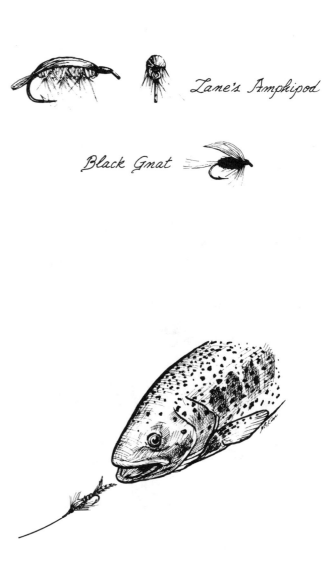

Lane's Amphipod

Black Gnat

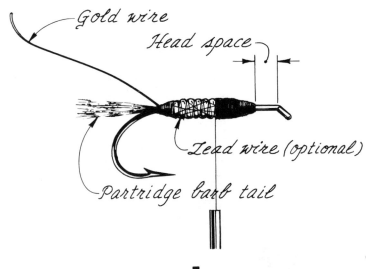

Gold wire

Head space

Lead wire (optional)

Partridge barb tail

1

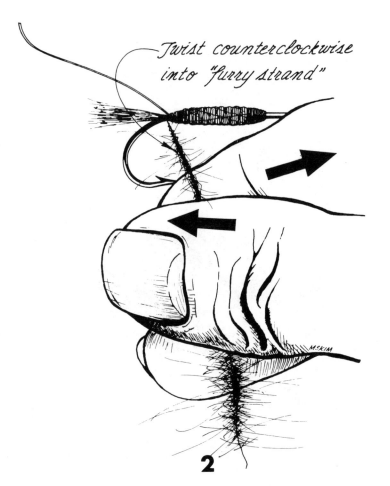

Twist counterclockwise into "furry strand"

2

Lowe's Grey Nymph

Type: Nymph

Simulates: Aquatic insect, immature form

Habitat: Freshwater streams, lakes, ponds

Takes: Trout, steelhead, bass and panfish

Background: This nymph was developed by Allen Lowe, Long Beach, California, starting with frustration on an eastern High Sierra stream, a pair of fingernail clippers and a "Gold Ribbed Hare's Ear Nymph." Since perfected, it has become a standard favorite among many western fly fishermen. Tied in Size 6 it has proved effective for tempting Trinity River steelhead. It should be tied in a variety of sizes, both unweighted and weighted.

Materials:

Hook: Sizes 6, 8, 10-16 Mustad #3906 TDE Bronzed

Thread: Size "A" to 6/0 Nylon, Black

Tail: Partridge (or Grouse) Breast Feather Barbs

Body: Weighted — Small Diameter Lead Wire. Mixed Muskrat and Mink, Dubbed

Rib: Fine Gold Wire, reverse spiral

Beard:. Partridge (or Grouse) Breast Feather Barbs

Head: Tying Thread

1. Leave head space. Wrap to the bend and tie in a 6-8 barb tail. Tie in a length of gold wire. On the weighted version, wrap 6-8 turns of lead wire at mid-shank, secure down with thread and form an evenly tapered underbody. Do not crowd the head space.

2. Apply dubbing wax to the first few inches of thread, then wipe the excess wax from your dubbing needle on the underbody. By hand or with a kitchen blender thoroughly separate and mix the body underfur and guard hairs into a loose mass. Apply fur sparsely along the waxed tying thread and, using thumb and forefinger (or the dubbing loop technique illustrated in Chapter IV) twist counterclockwise to form a furry strand.

3. Form a tapered body with the dubbed strand and tie it securely at the head space. Remove excess fur remaining on the tying thread (or clip off the excess loop, if the loop technique is used). Rib the body with gold wire in the reverse direction. This keeps the ribbing exposed and anchors the dubbed body. Tie off and trim excess wire.

4. Tie in 6-10 barbs for the beard (using the method illustrated in Chapter IV, or by reorienting the hook upside down in the vise), tie off and trim away the excess butts.

5. Form a relatively large head, whip finish and clip the tying thread. Apply head cement, making sure to clear the eye of hardened cement. On weighted versions it's a good idea to paint a dot of white or yellow lacquer atop the head for easier identification in the field.

Note that ribbing is reversed

3

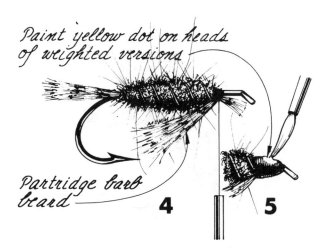

Paint yellow dot on heads of weighted versions

Partridge barb beard

4   **5**

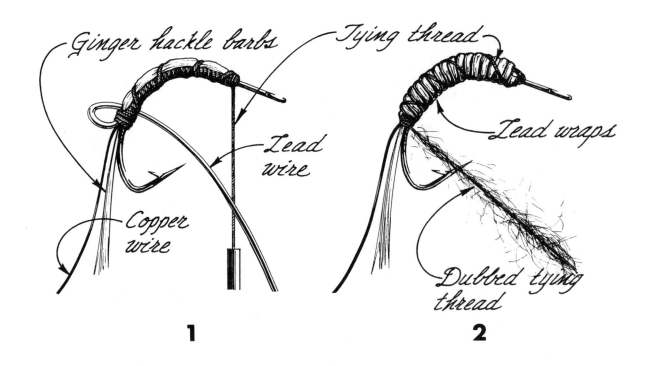

1

2

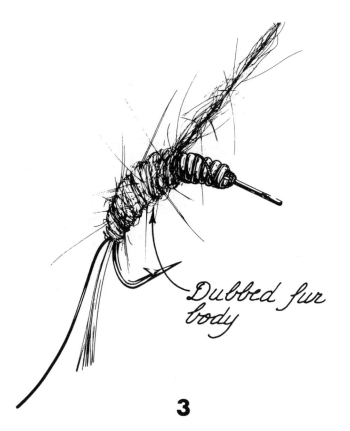

3

PATTERN NO. 7

Cross Fox Nymph

Type: Nymph-like Wet Fly

Simulates: Scud (Amphipod Crustacean)

Habitat: Freshwater rivers, streams

Takes: Trout

Background: This fly was originated by W.D. Hess of Montrose, Colorado, to imitate the scud found in Cheeseman Canyon, along the South Platte River. It has since been found effective for trout in the Green River, Wyoming, and the Gunnison River in Colorado. The name, "Cross Fox," derives from the type of fur used to dub the body, a color phase of the Red Fox.

Materials:

Hook: Sizes 12-14 Plated English Bait Hook
Thread: Size 6/0 Nylon, Black
Tail: Ginger Hackle Barbs
Weight: Fine Diameter Lead Wire
Ribbing: Fine Copper Wire
Body: Cross Fox Body Fur, (or Cream Underfur with Guard Hairs)
Legs: Ginger Hackle, Spun and Trimmed
Head: Tying Thread

1. Leave head space. Wrap thread to the hook's bend or slightly below. Tie in the tail, leaving excess barbs atop the shank. Tie in 2-inch lengths of copper and lead wire respectfully, then wrap down the excess hackle barbs to the head space. Wrap lead wire to near the head space and trim off the excess lead.

2. Secure the lead with thread back to the tail. Apply dubbing wax to the thread, then a mixture of underfur and guard hairs. Twist to form a dubbing strand, sparsely dubbed near the hook.

3. Form a dubbed body, tapering larger from the tail to head space.

4. Spiral the copper wire forward to form a fairly wide-spaced rib. Secure and trim off the excess. Tie in a hackle with barbs approximately body length behind the head space. Spin fully, tie off and trim the excess tip.

Spun hackle
Copper rib

4

5. Whip finish a small head, clip the thread and apply head cement.

6. Trim off the hackle barbs on the top and sides, leaving the lower barbs to act as "legs." Pick out the guard hairs on the body; the finished fly should have a shaggy look.

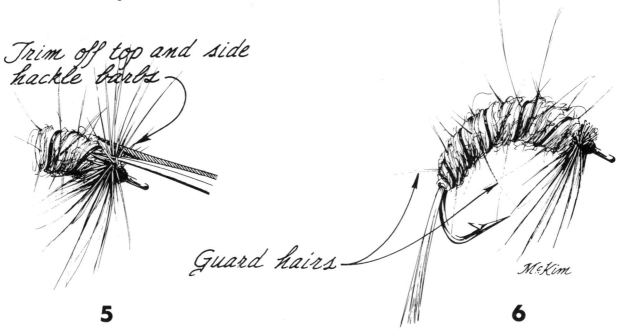

Trim off top and side hackle barbs

Guard hairs

5

McKim

6

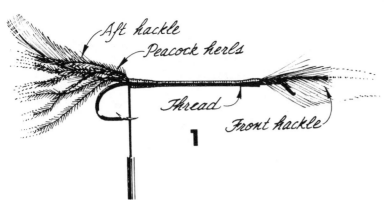

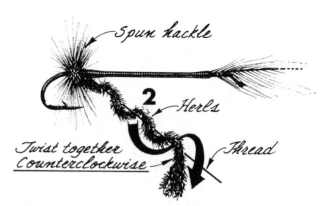

PATTERN NO. 8

Warden's Worry

Type: Wet Fly

Simulates: (Not Known)

Habitat: Freshwater Lakes, Streams

Takes: Trout and Panfish

Background: According to legend, this fly acquired its name only after the late A.L. Cupp of Chama, New Mexico unleashed his creation on the trout of southern Colorado and northern New Mexico. And if you entertain doubts that the game wardens in those areas were soon run ragged checking limits of trout, try this: tie the "Warden's Worry" and offer it to rainbows and browns wherever you find them. If all you have in your fishing neighborhood are bluegills and crappie, don't despair. The "Warden's Worry" works equally well on panfish.

How such a simple pattern as Mr. Cupp's could be improved is hard to imagine, but by spinning both hackles in brown, Harris E. "Bob" Streety of Mesa, Arizona has made it even more devastating. Be sure to tie some of each variation, both weighted and nonweighted.

Materials:
Hook: Sizes 8, 6 Mustad #79580 or #94720 TDE
Thread: Size "A" or 3/0 — Black
Weight: Lead Wire (Optional)
Fore Hackle: Neck Hackle, Brown, Spun
Aft Hackle: Neck Hackle, Grey (or Brown), Spun
Body: Peacock Herl
Head: Tying Thread

1. Leave ample head space. Tie the Fore Hackle atop the shank, concave side down, tip beyond the eye. Wrap back and tie in the Aft Hackle at the bend, concave side up, tip toward the rear. Tie in 4 to 6 long green peacock herls atop the Aft Hackle base.

2. Hold the herls out of the way and spin the Aft Hackle fully. Tie down and clip the excess tip. Wind the tying thread and herls together as shown to form a loosely twisted strand.

3. Coat the thread-wrapped shank with thinned head cement, then wrap the thread/herl strand forward over the wet shank to form a smooth, even body. Tie down at the Fore Hackle and remove the excess herl tips, if any. It may be that in your case the thread/herl strand was too short to completely cover the shank. If that happens, simply tie in additional herl, twist and proceed as before.

4. Spin the Fore Hackle fully, tie down and clip the excess hackle tip. Form a tapered head, whip finish and coat with head cement. Clear the eye.

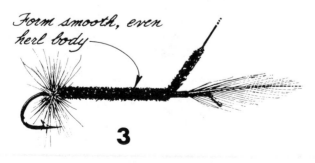

What's A Steelhead?

A good question, one frequently asked by beginners. Most are surprised by the answer: a steelhead is a rainbow trout that goes to sea. That's right. Even fisheries biologists cannot detect a difference between a so-called "resident" rainbow and a young steelhead that has yet to migrate into saltwater. Both appear identical at that stage. Why one fish should elect to travel while the other remains behind can only be attributed to instinct. Of course, steelhead ascending streams to spawn appear different from their resident cousins. For one thing, they're larger — and stronger. For another, the characteristic red stripe along each side of the rainbow is lacking in fresh run fish; they're dark on top with white underbellies and silvery sides. A steelhead's flesh is pinkish, not white.

Why the changes? Simple. It's just Mother Nature's camouflage. The fish are larger and stronger because the ocean is a superior source of protein, and in the open ocean dark colored backs are less visible to predators from above, while light sides and undersides are equally hard to see against the brighter background of the sky. The flesh gets its pink tinge from carotine, a substance produced by the crustaceans which form a large part of the steelhead's marine diet.

Steelhead are "anadromous" trout; that is, fish who live out their lives in the ocean and return only periodically to spawn. They also spend their first months or a year after birth in freshwater. Other anadromous species of particular interest to the fly fisherman include Atlantic and Pacific salmon, striped bass, shad, sea-run cutthroat and brown trout.

While some anadromous species cease to eat after they reenter freshwater (salmon and shad, for example), steelhead do feed upon the eggs deposited by spawning salmon. And yet, all the anadromous species cited are susceptible to the right artificial fly. Why a fish who refuses to eat in freshwater will strike a fly is still a mystery. Some believe that such strikes are a conditioned reflex, normal behavior during their years at sea in search of food. Others see it as an act of pure aggression (i.e., the fly has invaded its "turf," is therefore attacked). Whatever the truth, from the fly fisherman's standpoint it's a happy fact, and the patterns developed to press the advantage are numerous and varied.

Most steelhead-type flies are sinking patterns of the so-called "attractor" class. Such bright streamers, bucktails and wet flies perhaps remind the fish of preferred marine forage species. Some patterns, reminiscent of salmon eggs, obviously are meant to appeal to the steelhead's spawning tastes. Few if any dry patterns are tied; rarely, if ever, will steelhead rise to a dry.

Flies for anadromous species are seldom universally productive. Tastes vary from species to species and with the fish in different locales, often between the same fish in adjacent stream systems. That's why it's a safer bet to start with the patterns already proven successful on the river you plan to fish. Check with local tackle dealers and guides. Still it won't hurt to carry along some of the steelhead and other patterns in this book just in case. I caught my first steelhead on the **"Lowe's Grey Nymph"** (Pattern No. 6), a chance selection and a fly not previously known to tempt steelies.

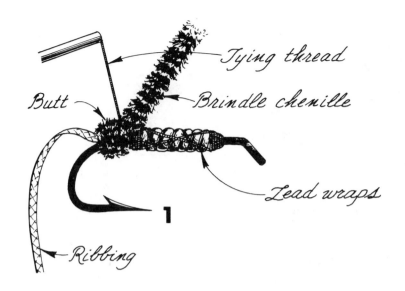

Tying thread
Butt
Brindle chenille
Lead wraps
Ribbing

1

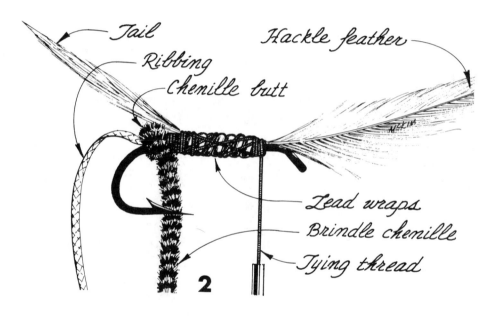

Tail
Hackle feather
Ribbing
Chenille butt
Lead wraps
Brindle chenille
Tying thread

2

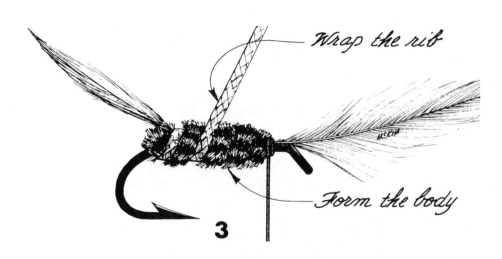

Wrap the rib
Form the body

3

PATTERN NO. 9

Brindle Bug

Type: Wet Fly, Steelhead Type

Simulates: (Not known)

Habitat: Freshwater northcoast rivers

Takes: Anadromous rainbow trout (steelhead)

Background: The originator of this fly is not known. It is an extremely effective pattern and one of the standards used throughout the Klamath/Trinity River system in northern California.

Materials:
Hook: Sizes 4, 6, 8 Forged Steelhead, Bronzed
Thread: Size 3/0 Nylon, Black
Rib: Silver Tinsel, Embossed
Body: Variegated Chenille; Black-Yellow or
    Brown-Green-Yellow
Weight: Lead Wire
Tail: One Small Brown Neck Hackle
Hackle: Brown Hackle, Spun, Wet
Head: Tying Thread

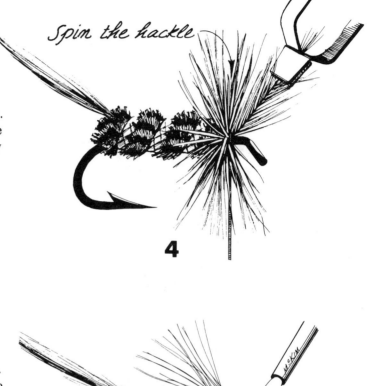

1. Leave head space and wrap to the hook's bend. Tie in a length of tinsel for the rib, then chenille for the body. Apply lead wraps along the shank and tie down securely with tying thread. Take one complete turn of chenille at the bend to form the butt and tie down. Do not trim excess chenille.

2. Tie in the tail atop the shank next to the butt, concave side up, tip toward the rear. Advance the thread to the head space and tie in the hackle feather, concave side up, tip forward of the eye.

3. Coat the shank with head cement and wrap a chenille body. Tie off and trim the excess chenille. Rib the body with 3 turns of tinsel, tie off at the head space and trim the excess tinsel.

4. Spin the hackle feather fully. Tie off and trim away the excess tip.

5. Form a large head, wrapping back on the spun hackle barbs so they sweep toward the rear, wet style. Whip finish and clip the tying thread. Coat the head with head cement.

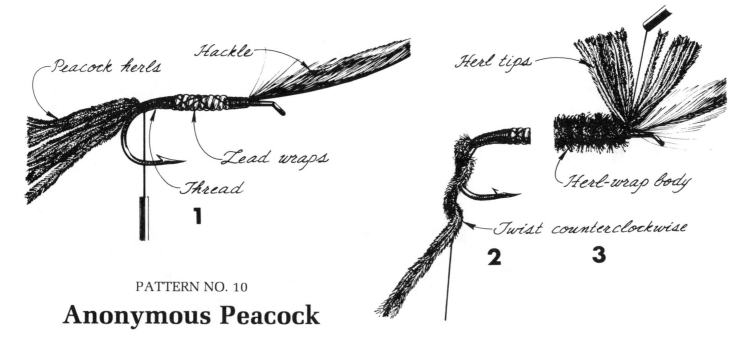

1

Labels: Peacock herls, Hackle, Lead wraps, Thread

Labels: Herl tips, Herl-wrap body, Twist counterclockwise

2　　**3**

PATTERN NO. 10

Anonymous Peacock

Type: Wet Fly, Steelhead Type

Simulates: (Not known)

Habitat: Freshwater northcoast rivers

Takes: Anadromous rainbow trout (steelhead)

Background: Of all the patterns designed for
  steelhead, this must be one of the simplest to tie.
  You should have little difficulty. I don't know
  who originated this fly, but according to Dan
  Sundberg, of Arcata, California, who is part
  Klamath Indian and runs a fishing guide service
  on the river of that name, it has proved itself to
  be a very good fly.

Materials:

  Hook: Sizes 6, 8 Mustad #7958 TDE Brz., or equal
  Thread: Size "A" Nylon, Black
  Body: 10 to 12 Peacock Herls
  Weight: Small Diameter Lead Wire
  Hackle: Black or Brown, Spun Wet Style
  Wings: Excess Herl Tips
  Head: Tying Thread

1. Leave ample head space. Wrap to slightly beyond
   the bend. Tie in 10 to 12 herls by their butts where
   thread wraps end. Weight the midshank with 5 to
   8 wraps of lead wire, secure in place with thread
   and tie in the hackle feather behind the head,
   concave side up, tip forward. Return thread to the
   bend and half-hitch.

2. Wrap the herls and tying thread together as
   shown to form a reinforced strand of body
   material.

3. Wrap the herl strand forward to form a tapering
   body. Untwist the excess tips at the head space.
   Do not trim off excess tips. Secure to shank
   behind the head.

4. Wrap the excess herl tips to extend backward as
   the fly's wing. Trim to length shown, if required.

5. Spin the hackle and wrap to sweep backward wet
   style. Form a medium sized head, whip finish
   and coat with clear head cement. Clear the eye of
   dried cement.

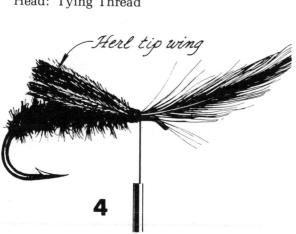

Label: Herl tip wing

4

Label: Spun hackle

5

Streamers and Bucktails

In freshwater, insects of many kinds are the major source of food for young fish. (The reverse is also true: fish fry often fall prey to large aquatic insects.) But as the fish grows it requires increasingly greater amounts of protein just to keep from starving. And while large trout, for example, continue to eat insects whenever available, the bulk of their diet consists of fish smaller than themselves. In saltwater, of course, nearly all gamefish species (once past the larval stage) subsist entirely on small fish, squid and other fast swimming forage. It's this taste for baitfish which justifies the existence of streamer flies and bucktails.

All streamer type flies, of which the so-called "bucktail" is a variation, are attempts to satisfy this preference. Imitations of every species imaginable have already been designed, with new ones utilizing the products of modern technology being introduced and tried each year.

By definition, a "streamer" is a baitfish imitation in which the shape is delineated by feathers; a "bucktail" gets its silhouette from the use of deer or other types of long hairs. In practice, few patterns are strictly one or the other. Many use both feathers and hair. The "**Snake Fly**" (Pattern No. 13) for example, while classed a "bucktail" uses a herl overwing; the barbs from a peacock tail feather. The "**Black Nosed Dace**" (Pattern No. 11) is an exception, a pure "bucktail." Conversely, the "**Hornberg**" (Pattern No. 12) is purely streamer; all feather wings.

The distinction between the two types of flies is unimportant. Under the right conditions both take fish of many kinds.

Lopez Sculpin

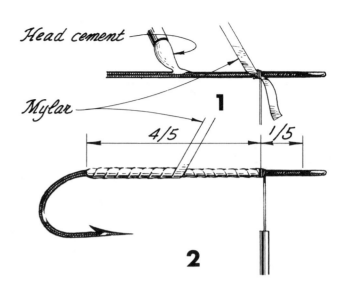

PATTERN NO. 11

Black Nosed Dace

Type: Bucktail

Simulates: Small freshwater bait fish

Habitat: Freshwater lakes, rivers and streams

Takes: Trout

Background: This fly, originated by Keith C. Fulsher of New York in the early 1960's, is one version of a basic pattern called the "Thunder Creek Series." It simulates a small minnow-like fish, the Dace, found primarily in the eastern part of the country. However, this has been proven to be an extremely effective fly wherever it has been used in waters in which small fish form a basic staple of the diet. It is also an effective pattern for saltwater species. Other flies in the "Thunder Creek Series" are essentially variations of colors and markings.

Materials:
Hook: Sizes 4/0 thru 12, 6XL RE
Thread: Size "A" Nylon, Red
Body: Silver Mylar Tinsel, Sized to Hook
Underwing: Black Bucktail
Wing: Brown Bucktail
Beard: White Bucktail
Gills: Red Tying Thread
Head: Bucktail
Eyes: Model Paints; Yellow with Black Pupil

1. Leave head space and tie in mylar. Coat the shank with head cement and, while wet, wrap the mylar smoothly to the bend.

2. Reverse direction and wrap the mylar back to the head space. Tie off and trim away the excess mylar.

3. Tie a sparse clump of black bucktail atop the hook, tips toward the rear. Trim the hair butts at a taper, then wrap the thread tightly to the eye of the hook, covering the butts.

4. Tie in a sparse clump of brown bucktail, tips extending beyond the eye and trim the hair butts at a taper. Wrap the thread tightly back to the mylar, covering the tapered butts.

5. Turn the hook upside down in the vise. Using the same procedure as with the brown overwing, tie in the white bucktail beard, tips extending beyond the eye a distance equal to the brown overwing. Taper the butts and wrap the thread tightly back to the mylar, covering the butts.

6. Fold the white bucktail beard back under the shank and secure it with tying thread at the start of the mylar body. Half-hitch. Reverse the position of the hook in the vise and repeat the same procedure with the overwing.

7. Whip finish with tying thread to form red gills. Clip thread. Brown bucktail should cover the top half of the head; white bucktail the bottom half. Coat the head several times with head cement and let dry. Paint a large yellow eye with a black pupil on opposing sides of the head. When dry, coat the head and gills with clear 2 part epoxy.

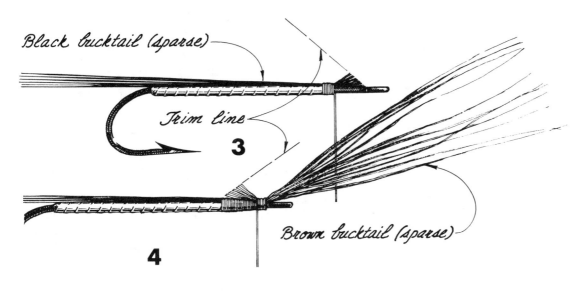

Black bucktail (sparse)

Trim line

3

4

Brown bucktail (sparse)

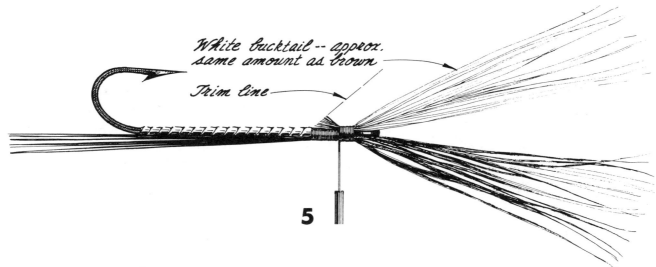

White bucktail -- approx.
same amount as brown

Trim line

5

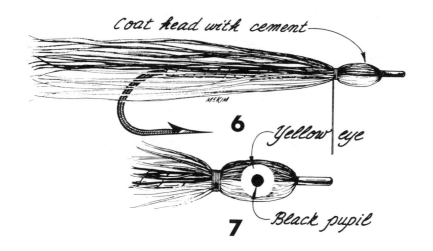

Coat head with cement

MCKIM

6

Yellow eye

7

Black pupil

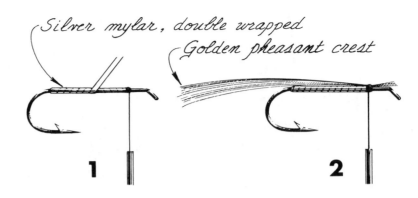

Silver mylar, double wrapped
Golden pheasant crest

1　　**2**

PATTERN NO. 12

Hornberg

Type: Streamer (also fished as a dry)

Simulates: Small minnow

Habitat: Freshwater streams, lakes

Takes: Trout and panfish

Background: This streamer fly was originated by
retired Conservation Warden Frank Hornberg of
Portage County, Wisconsin. The "Hornberg" is
the eastern version. The "Hornberg Special"
used in the west differs in having the tips of the
mallard wings lacquered together. Both flies are
excellent for trout and panfish.

Originally, the pattern called for Jungle Cock
Eye shoulders. Since this material can no longer
be obtained, various alternatives, including
plastic, are used as substitutes. I've found a
trimmed Guinea Fowl hackle with a painted dot
of yellow lacquer makes an effective imitation.
Some versions use slim yellow hackles for the
underwing, some use yellow hair, some golden
pheasant crest, as shown.

The fly is often fished dry until it sinks, and is
then retrieved as a streamer.

Materials:
Hook: Sizes 4-14 3XL Mustad #9672 TDE Bronzed
Thread: Size "A" Nylon, Black
Body: Silver Mylar or Flat Silver Tinsel
Underwing: Golden Pheasant Crest (or 2 Yellow
Neck Hackles)
Overwings:. Mallard Flank Feathers, Barred, Grey
Shoulders: Guinea Fowl Hackles, painted and
trimmed
Hackle: 2 Neck Hackles, spun, Grizzly or Adams
Head: Tying Thread

1. Leave ample head space. Tie in a 6-inch length of
   silver mylar. Lacquer the shank and wrap the
   mylar smoothly to the bend. Reverse direction
   and wrap back to the head space. Tie off and clip
   excess mylar.

2. Tie the crest feather underwing atop the shank,
   concave side down, tip extending to the rear. The
   underwing should be equal to twice the hook's
   length. (Or, cement together the tips of paired
   slim yellow neck hackles, concave sides together,
   and tie in such a way that the body is
   "sandwiched" between.)

3. Select a pair of matching mallard flank feathers
   and trim off the barbs near their butts. Tie in each
   wing separately, concave side facing and parallel
   to the body. Trim off the excess butts. The
   overwings should approximately equal the
   length of the underwing.

4. Select two guinea fowl hackles with distinct
   white and dark markings. Coat one side of each
   feather with thinned head cement or thinned
   pliobond glue and let thoroughly dry. Paint the
   white spot near the tip with yellow lacquer. Let
   dry.

5. Trim both feathers to match in size to the shape
   shown.

6. Tie the two imitation "Jungle Cock Eye"
   shoulders along both sides over the overwings at
   the back of the head space as shown. Trim the
   excess butts.

7. Tie in two dry neck hackles at the back of the head
   space. Spin each hackle feather separately and tie
   off. Trim their excess tips. Form a small tying
   thread head, whip finish and clip the thread.
   Apply thinned head cement to the head and the
   base of the spun hackles. Clear the eye of
   hardened cement. (For the "Hornberg Special,"
   cement the tips of the mallard overwings together
   and hold until dry.)

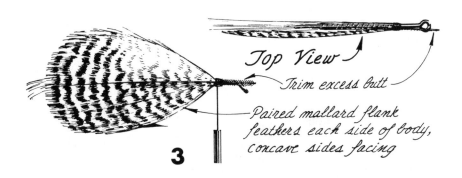

Top View

Trim excess butt

Paired mallard flank feathers each side of body, concave sides facing

3

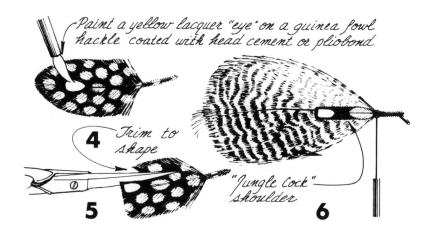

Paint a yellow lacquer "eye" on a guinea fowl hackle coated with head cement or pliobond

4 *Trim to shape*

5

"Jungle Cock" shoulder

6

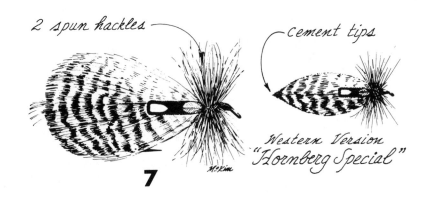

2 spun hackles

cement tips

7

Western Version "Hornberg Special"

M. Kim

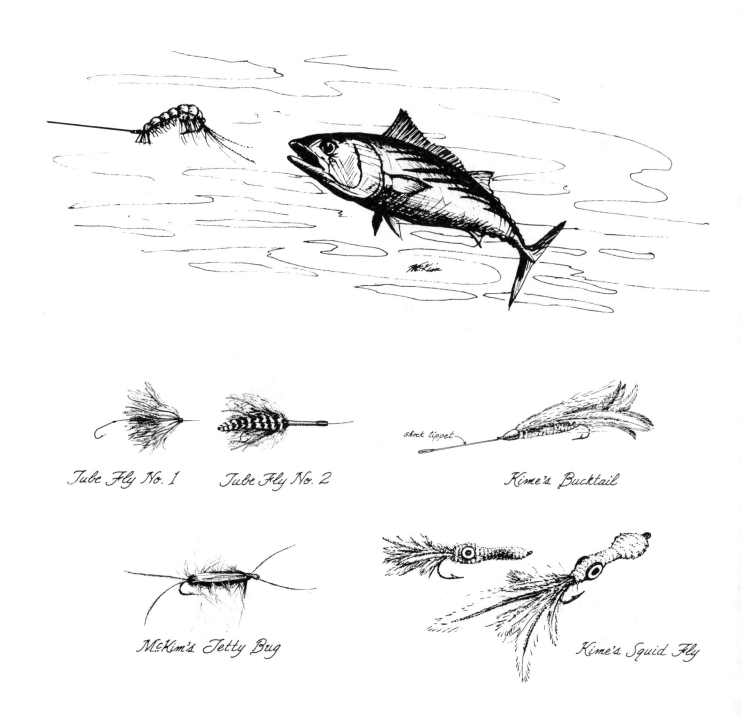

Tube Fly No. 1   Tube Fly No. 2   shock tippet   Kime's Bucktail

McKim's Jetty Bug   Kime's Squid Fly

Some types of saltwater flies.

Flies In The Salt?
You're Kidding!

It may come as a shock, but saltwater fly fishing is alive and well. You might say it has reached its adolescent years. And that's the most remarkable thing of all. Strange as it may now seem, throughout the long history of the artificial fly it was assumed by inveterate fly fishermen that saltwater species would not take a fly. How they could make such an unwarranted assumption is difficult to see. Commercial fishermen for years took their catch on barbless hook "feathers," a type of simple fly. Hawaiians have long caught "Opelu," a small mackerel used as bait for tuna and marlin, on small white flies. Undoubtedly, innumerable variations on this theme have occurred throughout the world of angling. The fact that Atlantic salmon have for centuries been tempted by flies while ascending rivers should have been a dead giveaway. These anadromous fish, and others like them, which return to freshwater only to spawn and spend their first year or so as juveniles, live most of their lives in the salt. It stands to reason that if they'll accept a fly in the river they ought to do so at sea. Still, it has only been within the past two decades or so that strictly marine fish of many species have also been found susceptible to the fly. Bonito and bonefish, tuna and tarpon — the list grows longer each year. And pound-for-pound saltwater gamefish are stronger than their freshwater counterparts.

Not all fly fishing techniques are applicable, of course. The saltwater fish that will take a dry fly is virtually non-existent. But many will accept a bass popping bug chugged along the surface. Most saltwater fishing is done with streamers and bucktails, shrimp, eel and other imitations that simulate the types of forage they're used to feeding upon. Unfortunately, the oceans are devoid of mayflies, stoneflies and caddis. Other than that, the same type of equipment and presentation techniques employed for strong freshwater fish such as trout and bass, and the anadromous species (steelhead, shad, salmon, stripers, etc.) will work. A whole new inventory of patterns specifically designed for the salt have been introduced, with additional ones being added every year, but many of the same wet fly and streamer patterns will also produce in marine waters.

If you live near the ocean, don't ignore the possibilities at your doorstep. Tie the saltwater patterns in this book and others, then give them a try. You won't regret it.

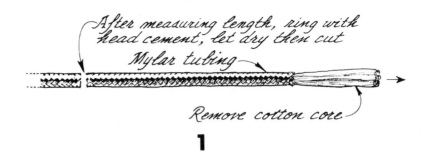

After measuring length, ring with head cement, let dry then cut

Mylar tubing

Remove cotton core

1

PATTERN NO. 13

Snake Fly

Type: Bucktail

Simulates: Anchovies and similar forage fish

Habitat: Saltwater

Takes: Bonito and other pelagic gamefish

Background: Origins not known, although this pattern is one of the earliest flies to employ a mylar tubing body. It is a very effective saltwater "streamer." A similar version tied with a second hook in tandem connected by a length of stout monofilament to the first helps to avoid the problems associated with "short striking" fish. The added weight, however, increases the difficulty of casting, and the fly is often trolled instead. This fly should be tied in several lengths and various color schemes to adjust to the sizes and colors of local baitfish.

Materials:

Hook: Size 2 to 2/0 XST, 3XS, RE, Bronzed or Tinned

Thread: Size "A" Nylon, White and Red

Tail: White Bucktail

Body: Silver Mylar Tubing, Core Removed

Underwing: White under Black Bucktail, 4 inch minimum

Overwing: Green Peacock Herl

Head: Red Tying Thread

Eyes: Painted — White Iris, Black Pupil

1. Mark a 3 inch length of mylar tubing with head cement. Cut at the marks and remove and discard the yarn core.

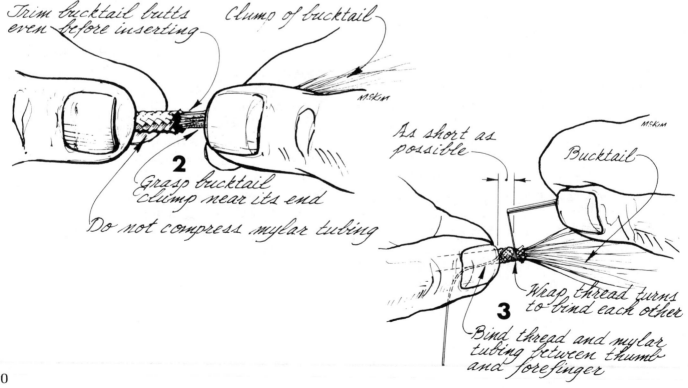

Trim bucktail butts even before inserting

Clump of bucktail

2

Grasp bucktail clump near its end

Do not compress mylar tubing

As short as possible

Bucktail

3

Wrap thread turns to bind each other

Bind thread and mylar tubing between thumb and forefinger

100

2. Insert a clump of white bucktail into one end. Tail should be 1½ inches long. Trim the butt end of the hair clump and grasp it tightly near its end. This will make the task of inserting the butt ends of the hairs into the mylar tube easier. If you still have difficulty, try moistening the clump end with head cement or rubber-type glue, compress together then insert.

3. Grasp the mylar tubing near the end. Squeeze to bind the bucktail clump. Bind the free end of the white tying thread between your thumb and the mylar, tie the jamb knot and continue wrapping until a smooth transition is formed.

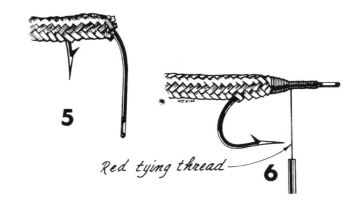

Red tying thread

White bucktail
Coat with head cement

4. Whip finish, clip thread and cement the thread wraps.

5. Sharpen the hook's point with an auto point file or hone. Insert the point into the open end of the mylar tubing and out the side.

6. Place the hook in the vise. Wrap the shank with red tying thread, then liberally coat the wraps with head cement and tie down the mylar ¼ inch from the eye. This leaves sufficient head space.

7. Tie down in sequence atop the body — white bucktail, black bucktail, 6 to 8 peacock herls. These form the underwings and overwing of the fly and should be as long as possible, extending at least to the end of the tail.

8. Trim the excess butts at a taper and tie down. Form a large red tying thread head, whip finish and clip thread. Coat with head cement. Paint a large white eye with a black pupil on opposing sides of the head. When dry, coat the entire head with clear 2-part epoxy.

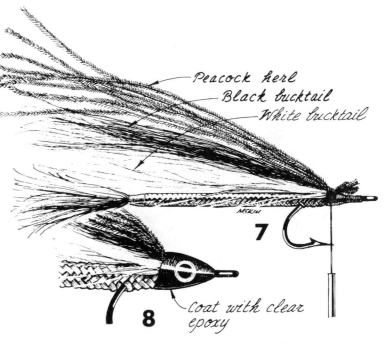

Peacock herl
Black bucktail
White bucktail

Coat with clear epoxy

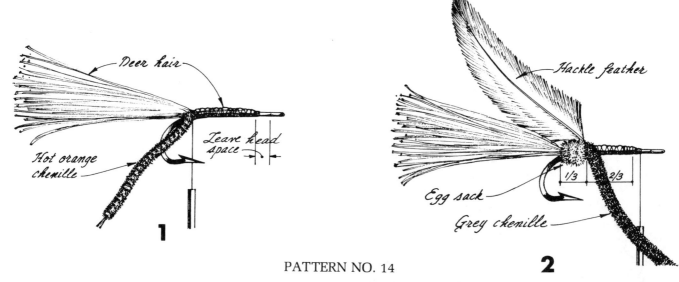

PATTERN NO. 14

Sand Crab

Type: Wet Fly, Saltwater type

Simulates: Sand Crab (Sand Flea, Sandbug, *Hippa talpoida*)

Habitat: Ocean surf zone

Takes: Surfperch, Corbina, Croaker, etc.

Background: This fly was originated by Ned Grey of Montrose, California, proprietor of Sierra Tackle, a fine source of quality fly tying materials. It is an effective imitation of a favorite food of various species inhabiting inshore beach waters, notably along the southern California coastline.

Materials:

Hook: Size 2, 4 Mustad #3407 Tinned, Forged, Ringed
Thread: Size "A" Nylon, Brown
Shellcase: Long Deer Body Hair, Natural Brown
Egg Sack: Medium Diameter Chenille, Hot Orange
Legs:. Blue Dun Hackle, Palmered
Body: Large Diameter Chenille, Grey
Head: Tying Thread

1. Leave head space. Wrap to the hook's bend. Select a large clump of deer hair, trim off close to the skin, brush out the fuzz and even the tips in a hair tamper. Tie atop the hook, tips at the head space. Secure the hairs along the shank. Tie in a 2 inch length of hot orange chenille at the bend.

2. Wrap the rear ⅓ of the body with orange chenille to form the egg sack, tie off and trim the excess chenille. Tie in a large hackle feather, then a 4 inch length of grey chenille next to the egg sack.

3. Form the body with close wraps of grey chenille. Tie off at the rear of the head space and trim off the excess chenille. Palmer the body with hackle, tie off and trim off the feather's tip.

4. Bring the deer hair tightly forward atop the egg sack and body and tie the butts down at the start of the head space. Half-hitch. Trim the excess butts at a bevel.

5. Form a large head and whip finish. Trim off tying thread and coat the head with head cement or clear 2-part epoxy.

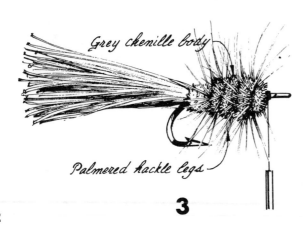

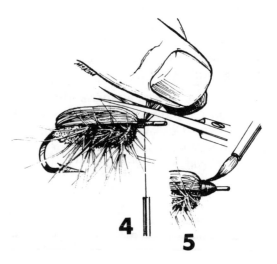

water's surface. Dry flies float because the surface film resists penetration and the surface area of the dry fly is large in proportion to its weight. This spreads the load and the fly bends but does not rupture the surface. If, however, water is absorbed by the fly, its weight is added and the wet materials tend to become part of the surface film, in which event the fly sinks. This explains why, from the fly tier's standpoint, dry patterns should always be constructed from materials possessing superior water resistive qualities, and when finished waterproofed with a high quality water repellent product.

Drying the fly by false casting, washing off fish slime (assuming your creation has demonstrated its worth) and other after-the-fact remedies, though effective, are lame substitutes for good fly tying practice.

Seeing Is Believing

Invisible fingers tease the bright fleck along its journey. A sudden swirl and the painstakingly crafted flotsam disappears, to be instantly replaced by taut line and shocked surprise. You react... or, if this most exciting scenario in fly fishing is a new experience, overreact. When that happens, the trout often as not regains its freedom with nothing more to show for the mistake than a sore lip and a dangling ornament. Or the trees and brush become the uncaring beneficiaries of your hours at the vise.

What makes this supreme thrill a reality? Several things — the trout's instinctive reaction to a pseudo-normal situation and the surface tension of water, plus the resistance to wetting of the materials from which you've constructed your fly. These form the foundation of dry fly fishing. The fly is accepted because the normal fare of freshwater fish is comprised of many types of winged insects on or hovering above the

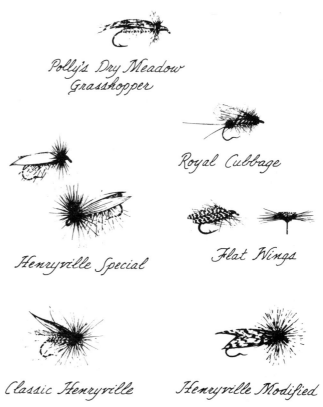

Polly's Dry Meadow Grasshopper

Royal Cubbage

Henryville Special

Flat Wings

Classic Henryville

Henryville Modified

Dry flies.

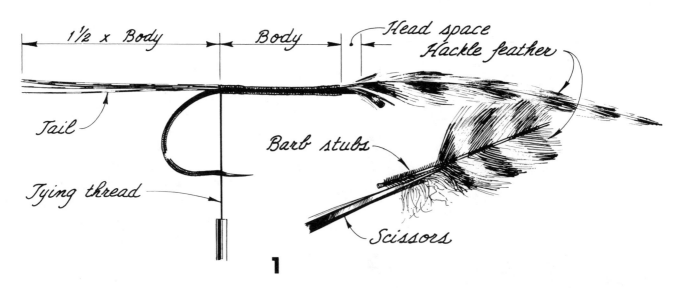

1

PATTERN NO. 15

Cheater Adams

Type: Dry Fly

Simulates: Adult Mayfly Dun

Habitat: Small streams, lakes and ponds

Takes: Trout, bluegills and other panfish

Background: This fly, an adaptation of the classic "Adams" dry fly, is the innovation of James R. Eriser, two times president of the Federation of Fly Fishermen, and a first class fly tier and fly fisherman.

Ever since I've known Jim he has always been an extremely busy guy (something that retirement along the Deschutes in Oregon has not changed). So when time came for fishin' and his fly box was low, he wasn't above abbreviating his flies for "the Gorge." That's the fabulous 7 mile stretch of Brown Trout water on the Owens River below Crowley Lake in the Eastern High Sierra. Hence the name "Cheater" Adams. It's been said "any fly will work in the High Sierra as long as it's grey and Size 16 or smaller!" The "Adams" (which was originally a *caddis* imitation) and Jim's "Cheater" version fit that specification. Both are very effective; one is just simpler to tie.

Materials:

Hook: Sizes 12-18 Mustad #94845 Barbless, or #94840 TDE, or #94842 TUE Dry Fly Hook
Thread: Sizes 6/0-8/0 Nylon, Black
Hackle: Cree Variant, Neck, Dry Quality
Tail: Cree Variant Hackle Barbs, Dry Quality
Body: Muskrat Body Fur, Dubbed
Head: Tying Thread

1. Leave head space. Using scissors, trim the barbs close to the quill near the butt of the hackle feather. Tie the hackle atop the shank, tip forward, concave side down. Wrap the tying thread toward the hook's bend. Select 4 to 6 stiff Cree hackle barbs and tie in to form the tail.

2. Apply dubbing wax to the tying thread. Thoroughly mix muskrat fur by hand or in a kitchen blender and apply sparsely to the thread. Twist the thread/fur counterclockwise between thumb and forefinger to form a furry strand.

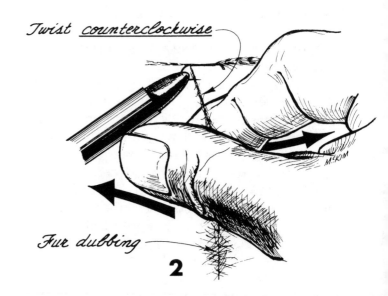

2

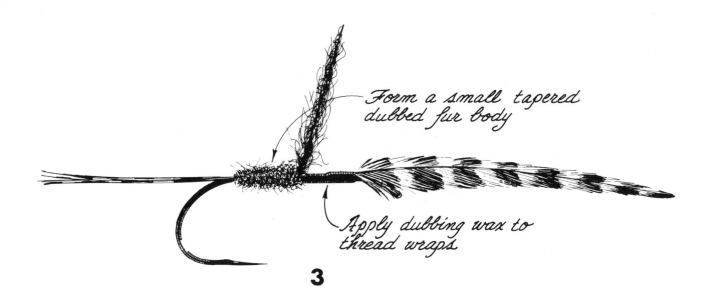

Form a small tapered dubbed fur body

Apply dubbing wax to thread wraps

3

3. Form a small, tightly wrapped dubbed fur body, tapering up toward the head space. Tie off at the head space. Clean the tying thread of all unused fur.

4. Using hackle pliers, wind the entire hackle feather in the rear half of the head space, leaving enough space for a small head. Tie off and remove the excess tip.

5. Whip finish the head and clip the tying thread. Saturate the head and the base of the spun hackle with thinned head cement. Clear the eye. When the fly is finished, treat the entire fly with a high quality liquid or spray water repellent.

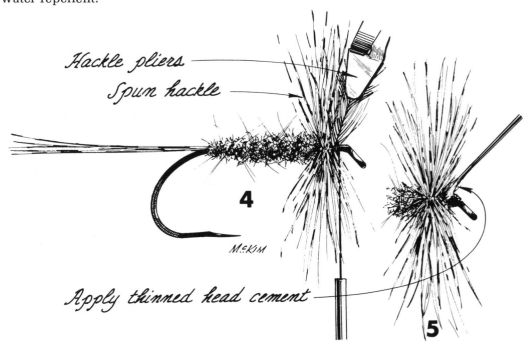

Hackle pliers
Spun hackle

4

M?KIM

Apply thinned head cement

5

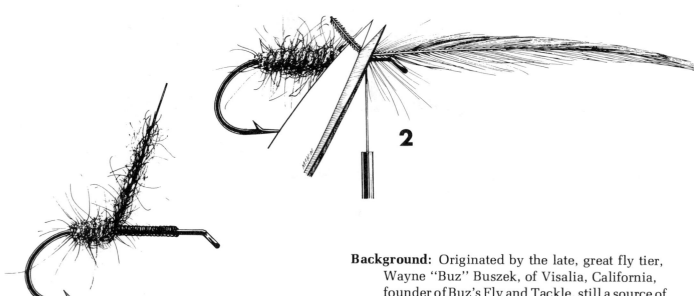

1

2

PATTERN NO. 16

Kings River Caddis

Type: Dry Fly

Simulates: Adult Caddisfly

Habitat: Freshwater streams

Takes: Trout

Background: Originated by the late, great fly tier, Wayne "Buz" Buszek, of Visalia, California, founder of Buz's Fly and Tackle, still a source of high quality flies and materials. Buz designed the pattern specifically for trout of the Kings River, an excellent trout stream draining the western High Sierra in California. Caddis are abundant and comprise a major source of food for its trout population. Since its introduction, this pattern has been proved effective throughout North America and elsewhere. There are several variations of the basic pattern, but I suspect the fly's abiding success really lies in its silhouette...and where, when and how it's fished.

Materials:

Hook: Sizes 10-16 Mustad #94840 TDE XF, Bronzed

Thread: Size 6/0-8/0 Nylon or Silk, Brown

Body: Raccoon Body Fur, Dubbed

Hackle: 1 or 2 Brown Neck Hackles, Dry Quality

Wings: Mottled Brown Turkey, Tied Tent Style

1. Leave head space. Wrap to the hook's bend. Wax 2-3 inches of tying thread and apply well mixed fur. After twisting counterclockwise to form a furry strand, form a rather large, shaggy body.

2. Trim off the fluff barbs near the butt of the hackle feather with scissors and tie atop the hook, tip forward, concave side down. Trim off the excess butt of the hackle.

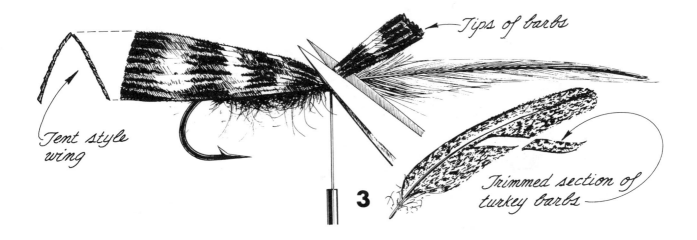

Tips of barbs

3

Tent style wing

Trimmed section of turkey barbs

3. Spray a mottled turkey wing feather with fixative, then with scissors cut out a section of barbs. Section should be about twice the width of the gap of the hook. Fold and tie atop the hook tent style, barb tips forward, butts to the rear. Tie in at the back of the head space. Trim the butts to slant downward toward the rear. The wing should extend approximately half the body's length beyond the bend. Trim off the excess tips at a taper.

4. Spin the hackle fully, tie off and trim or snap off the excess hackle tip.

5. Form a small head, whip finish and clip the tying thread. Coat the head and base of the hackle with thinned head cement. Clear the eye. Treat the entire finished fly with a high quality liquid or spray water repellent.

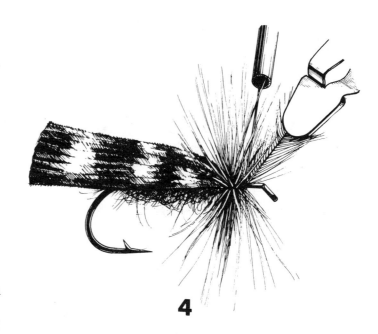

4

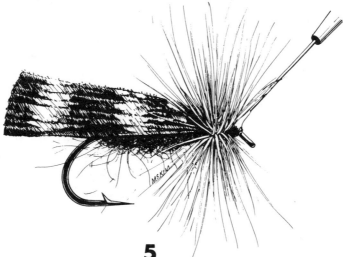

5

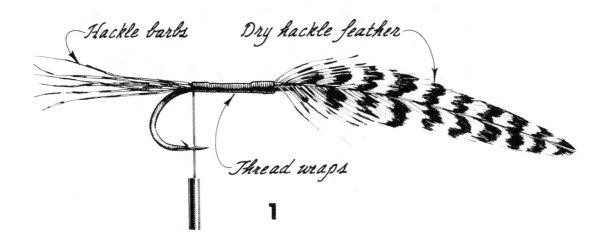

Hackle barbs   Dry hackle feather

Thread wraps

1

PATTERN NO. 17

McKim's Evadry

Simulates: Adult Mayfly or Fluttering Caddis

Habitat: Rivers, lakes and streams

Takes: Trout — other freshwater panfish

Background: So far as I know I am the first to use "Evazote" foam to provide positive dry fly buoyancy; a body material that offers exciting possibilities. In fact, tests indicate "Evazote"-tied dry flies just might float forever were it not for the drag of the leader and the absorptive qualities of other materials used in the fly's construction. Usually, brisk false casting will restore long lasting buoyancy; if not, you can always treat the fly with dry fly floatant. The true test, of course, is not how well it floats, but whether or not it produces. It does. Many of Arizona's White Mountain rainbows have already attested to that.

It's not a difficult fly, but don't be deceived by its apparent simplicity. Too little foam will not support the hook and other materials, too much distorts the fly's silhouette and too much foam stretched thin loses buoyancy.

Materials:

Hook: Sizes 12-18 Mustad #94840 TDE XF Bronzed

Thread: Size 6/0 to 8/0 Prewaxed — Brown or to suit

Hackle: One or Two Dry Quality Hackles, Spun Cree or Tier's Choice

Tail: Hackle Barbs, Dry Quality — Cree or Tier's Choice

Overbody: "Evazote" or fine closed cell Polythene Foam — White

Underbody: Seal-Ex or equal — Yellow — Dubbed

Head: Tying Thread

Overbody Color: Pantone-type Waterproof Marking Pens to Suit

1. Leave ample head space. Select one or two dry hackles (depending upon fly size). Tie atop shank, concave side down, tip beyond eye. Wrap back and tie 3 to 6 stiff hackle barbs at the bend for a tail 1½ to 2 times body length.

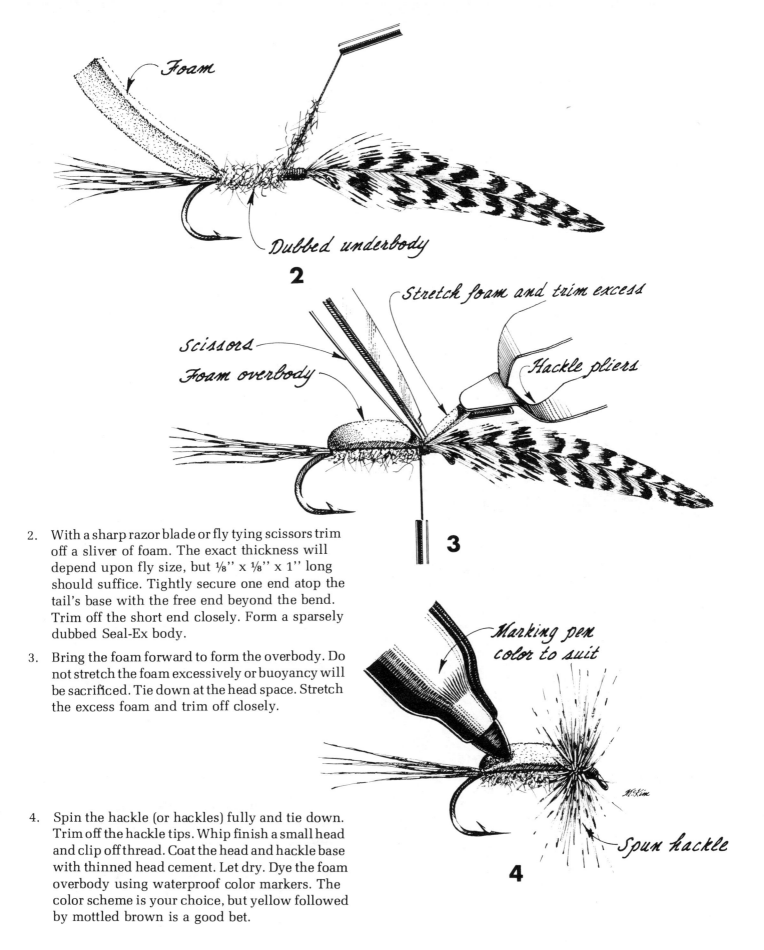

Foam

Dubbed underbody

2

Scissors

Foam overbody

Stretch foam and trim excess

Hackle pliers

3

Marking pen color to suit

Spun hackle

4

2. With a sharp razor blade or fly tying scissors trim off a sliver of foam. The exact thickness will depend upon fly size, but ⅛'' x ⅛'' x 1'' long should suffice. Tightly secure one end atop the tail's base with the free end beyond the bend. Trim off the short end closely. Form a sparsely dubbed Seal-Ex body.

3. Bring the foam forward to form the overbody. Do not stretch the foam excessively or buoyancy will be sacrificed. Tie down at the head space. Stretch the excess foam and trim off closely.

4. Spin the hackle (or hackles) fully and tie down. Trim off the hackle tips. Whip finish a small head and clip off thread. Coat the head and hackle base with thinned head cement. Let dry. Dye the foam overbody using waterproof color markers. The color scheme is your choice, but yellow followed by mottled brown is a good bet.

Humpy

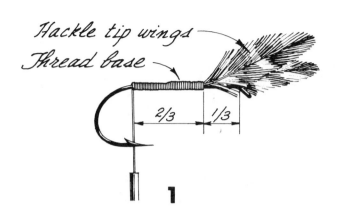

Hackle tip wings
Thread base

2/3   1/3

1

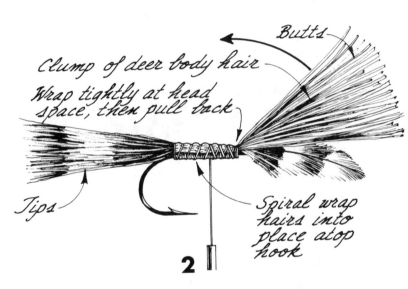

Butts

Clump of deer body hair
Wrap tightly at head
space, then pull back

Tips

Spiral wrap
hairs into
place atop
hook

2

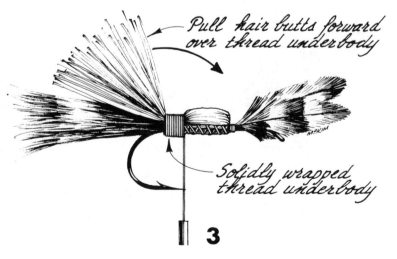

Pull hair butts forward
over thread underbody

Solidly wrapped
thread underbody

3

Type: Dry Fly

Simulates: Adult May Fly

Habitat: Rivers, streams and lakes

Takes: Trout and Panfish

Background: This is a variation of the famous "Humpy" that incorporates tying innovations by Clarence Tarbet of Long Beach, California. The "Humpy" is by far his favorite dry fly. The original pattern was called the "Horner Deer Hair," after its originator, the late great fly tier, Jack Horner of San Francisco, California. Later versions were renamed the "Humpy," probably because of the humped appearance of the deer hair overbody. This pattern is extremely productive on the Madison, Henry's Fork of the Snake and other trout streams in Idaho and Montana. However, in suitable sizes I have found it works nearly everywhere.

Materials:

Hook: Sizes 10-16 Mustad #94840 TDE XF Bronzed

Thread: Size "A" to 8/0 — Yellow

Wings: Grizzly Hackle Tips — Color of Overbody

Underbody: Tying Thread

Overbody: Deer Body Hair — Natural or Dyed

Hackle: 2 Dry Quality Hackles — either Grizzly, Mixed Grizzly and Brown, or Cree

1. Start the fly ⅓ shank length behind the eye. Select 2 hackle feather tips and tie them in at this point, tips forward and curved away from each other. Trim off the excess butts and wrap solidly to the hook's bend.

2. Select a clump of deer body hair about the thickness of a wooden match. The hairs should be as long and fine as possible with well defined tips. Clean out the fuzz and even up the tips in a hair tamper. Trim the butts to an even length. Tie the clump atop the hook, tips to the rear, making fairly loose wraps to forstall flaring of the tail. The tail should equal the distance from eye to hook bend. Wrap the tying thread to within 3 or 4 wraps of the wings, snugly secure the hairs at that point then spiral wrap back to the bend.

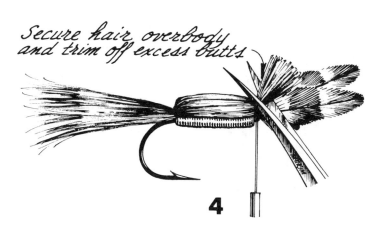

Secure hair overbody and trim off excess butts

4

3. Grasp the hair butts, pull them tightly back atop the hook and securely wrap them down at the base of the tail. Form an underbody of close consecutive wraps of tying thread. Stop at the wings.

4. Bring the deer hair butts forward over the underbody and tie them down securely behind the wings. Half-hitch, trim off the excess butts and apply a drop of head cement at the connection. Deer hair should cover the top and upper half of the fly's body.

5. Cock the wings upright, secure them in that position and figure "8" wrap them to splay apart. Select 2 dry fly hackles and tie them in front of the wings.

6. Spin each hackle individually behind and in front of the wings. Spin the hackles fully, filling the space between the wings and head. Tie off and trim away the excess tips.

7. Form a very small head — essentially nothing more than a whip finish — clip the thread and apply head cement. Clear the eye. Treat the entire fly with a quality moisture repellent liquid or spray and allow it to thoroughly dry.

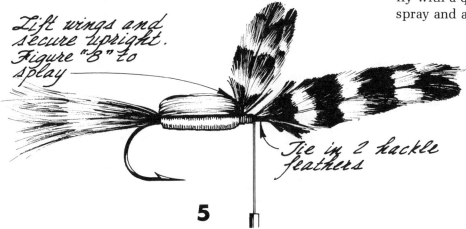

Lift wings and secure upright. Figure "8" to splay

Tie in 2 hackle feathers

5

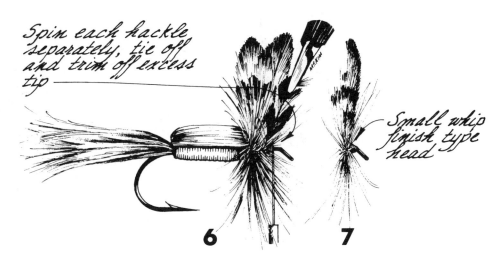

Spin each hackle separately, tie off and trim off excess tip

Small whip finish type head

6   **7**

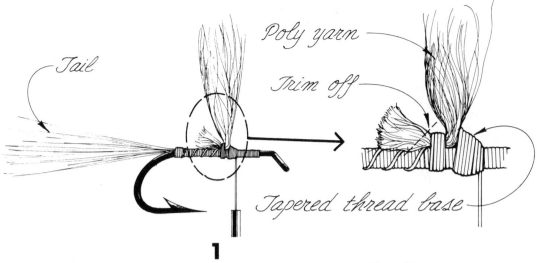

1

PATTERN NO. 19
Poly Mayfly

Type: Dry Fly

Simulates: Adult Mayfly, aquatic insect

Habitat: Freshwater streams, lakes, ponds

Takes: Trout

Background: The innovation incorporated into this otherwise standard dry fly is the wing material. To Grant Mounteer of Martinez, California, must go the credit for a uniquely lifelike mayfly wing made from "Poly Yarn," a material whose polypropylene fibers are highly water-resistant. The resulting fly is very durable, and combined with the "parachute" hackle, very stable and buoyant. Grant's wing forming technique can be used on any number of dry fly patterns besides the one illustrated.

Materials:

Hook: Sizes 10-16 Mustad #94840 TDE XF Bronzed

Thread: Sizes 6/0-8/0 Prewaxed Nylon, Color to Match Body

Tail: Neck Hackle Barbs, Brown, Dry Quality

Wing: "Poly Yarn," White

Body: Dubbed Fur, Cream Colored

Hackle: Neck Hackle, Brown, Dry Quality

Head: Tying Thread

1. Leave head space. Wrap to the bend and tie in the tail. Advance the thread to mid-shank and tie in a length of poly yarn with the longer length extending toward the eye. Secure its base with several wraps then lift the longer portion to the vertical and build a tapered thread base in front. Trim off the poly yarn butt.

2. Twist the yarn so the fibers are parallel to each other. Form a small loop and tie down the free end atop the thread base, then wrap 5-8 turns around the base of the loop. Half-hitch and trim the excess yarn butts. Spiral the thread back to the tail and apply fur dubbing.

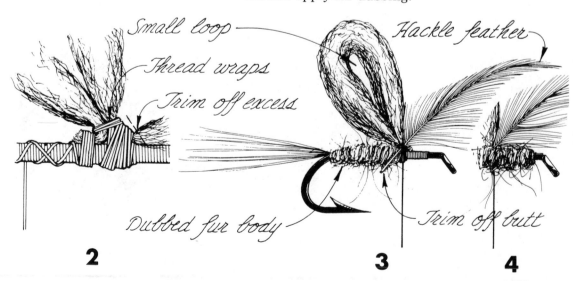

2   **3**   **4**

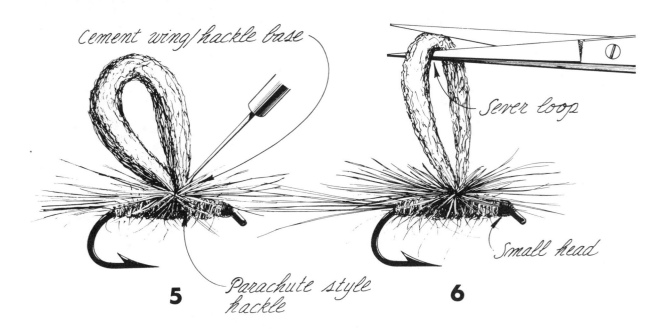

cement wing/hackle base

Sever loop

Small head

Parachute style
hackle

5   **6**

3. Form a dubbed fur body tapering up to the base of
   the wing. Tie in the hackle feather and trim off the
   excess butt.

4. Dub the fur body forward to the head space,
   half-hitch then loosely spiral the thread back to
   the base of the wing.

5. Spin the hackle 2-4 turns "parachute" style
   around the wing's base. Tie off and trim the
   excess tip. Loosely spiral the tying thread
   forward, form a small head and whip finish. Clip
   the tying thread and apply thinned head cement
   to the head and base of the wing/hackle.

6. Lift the poly yarn loop upright and sever it in two.

7. Use your bodkin to separate and comb out the
   poly yarn fibers.

8. Trim the wing to shape and apply thinned head
   cement to its leading edge. Let thoroughly dry.
   After the fly is finished, treat the entire fly with a
   high quality liquid or spray moisture repellent.

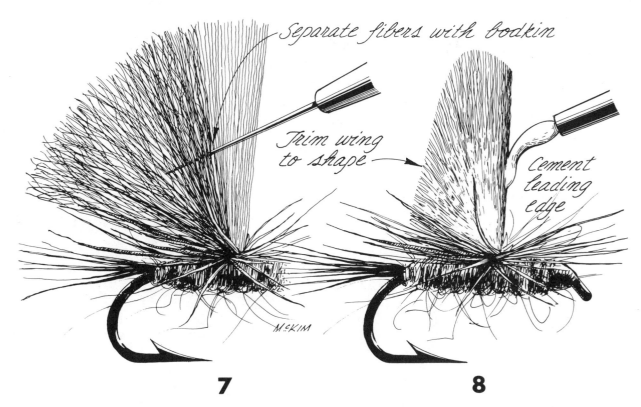

Separate fibers with bodkin

Trim wing
to shape

Cement
leading
edge

M?KIM

7   **8**

Fake Deacon

Black's Mouse

Nixon's Winged Poofer

Poppers

The popping bug is to the bass and bluegill flyrodder what the dry fly is to the dry fly addict. Visible fun. As to the eternal (or so it seems) argument between trout and bass anglers over the relative merits of their favorite species... no comment. But, no one can remain unaffected when a lunker bass (or even a scrappy little bluegill) slams a bug chugging the surface. There's just no delicacy at all at the take. A boil followed by sheer panic. With a bass's hard mouth and penchant for diving into weeds, drowned vegetation and the like, it's wise to use sharp hooks and set the hook as if you planned to "fillet him on the spot."

The secret of a well-made popping bug is sturdy construction coupled with a design that makes the fly "gurgle" or "pop" when it's being retrieved. It also helps to develop patience, the patience to let your bug sit awhile after casting, until the water quiets down. When it is still, start your retrieve. Wait. Twitch. Wait. Do that and you may soon be pleasantly surprised.

Popper bodies are made from several materials. Cork and deer body hair are two long time favorites. Balsa wood is another. "**Stoner's Bass Bug**" (Pattern No. 21) is an example of an excellently designed spun deer hair popping bug. Pattern No. 20 is a panfish popper constructed from polyethylene foam weatherstripping, a material which, to my knowledge, has not previously been used to make popper bodies. I believe, however, that once tiers begin to discover the potential of both polyethylene closed cell foams and the "Evazote" foam used for the bodies of my "**Evadry**" (Pattern No. 17) and "**Evafloat'n Frog**" (Pattern No. 24), the gamefish population will have much to choose from.

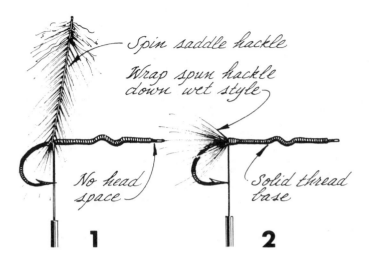

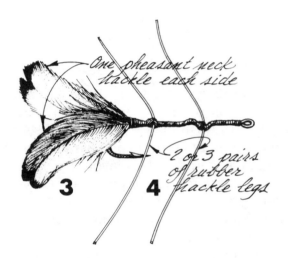

PATTERN NO. 20

McKim's Weatherbug

Type: Panfish Popper

Simulates: Large insect

Habitat: Freshwater lakes, ponds

Takes: Panfish, Bluegills, etc.

Background: I won't go so far as to call this fly a "pattern." It could be any small popper tied to conform to a relatively standard silhouette. The body could just as easily be made from cork, balsa or another material. And the tying sequence would remain essentially unchanged were you to use those materials. Whether or not other tiers have tried polythene closed cell foam for their popper bodies, I don't know. Maybe I was the first. The one thing I am sure of is that once the advantages of polythene-type foams are recognized I won't be the last. Polythene is tough, has an "alive" feel when squeezed, and floats like a dream. One package of weatherstripping will make all the panfish poppers you'll need for a long time to come.

Materials:
Hook: Sizes 8-14 Mustad #33903 or equal Popper Hook, Kink Shank RE
Thread: Size "A" Nylon — White
Tail: Red Saddle Hackle, Spun, with Brown Ringneck Pheasant Neck Hackle each side
Legs: Small Rubber Hackle
Body: ½"x⅜" Closed Cell Polyethylene (Polythene) Foam Strip Weatherstripping — White — Contact Adhesive One Face
Belly: Same as body
Cement: 5-minute 2-part Clear Epoxy Glue

1. Start back of the eye and wrap to the bend. Half-hitch. Tie in the saddle hackle by its tip. Spin fully.

2. Tie the hackle down and trim its excess tip. Wrap the thread back so hackle barbs lay wet style.

3. Tie a pheasant neck hackle on each side of the tail, concave side out, tip toward the rear.

4. Tie in rubber hackle legs, 2 or 3 each side. Allow ample length on both sides of the fly. The legs should be trimmed to the desired length after the body is in place. Whip finish and clip thread.

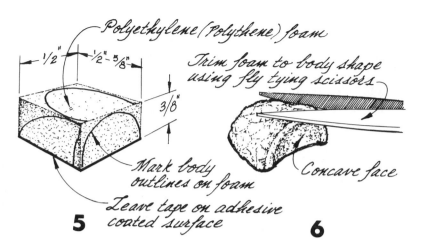

Polyethylene (Polythene) foam

1/2" 1/2" - 5/8" 3/8"

Trim foam to body shape using fly tying scissors

Mark body outlines on foam

Leave tape on adhesive coated surface

Concave face

5   **6**

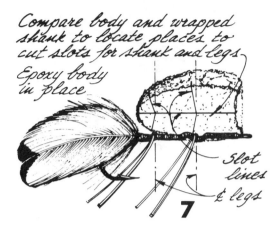

Compare body and wrapped shank to locate places to cut slots for shank and legs. Epoxy body in place.

Slot lines & legs

7

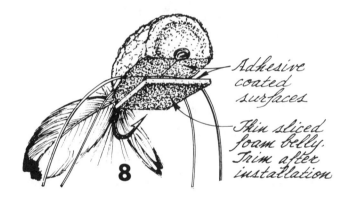

Adhesive coated surfaces

Thin sliced foam belly. Trim after installation

8

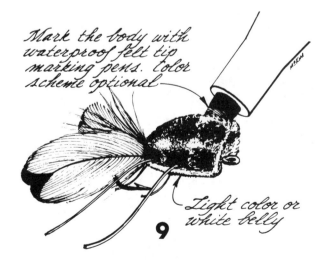

Mark the body with waterproof felt tip marking pens. Color scheme optional

Light color or white belly

9

5. Cut a length of polythene foam weatherstripping. Leave the tape covering the adhesive coated side in place. Mark the shape of the fly's body on the top, sides and end of the foam.

6. Use fly tying scissors to trim the body to shape. The body need not be overly smooth — a "hewn" surface enhances the fly's appearance.

7. Remove the protective tape covering and compare the body to the wrapped hook shank. With a ballpoint pen, lightly mark the positions of the legs on the underbody. Use a sharp razor blade to slice slots for the shank and legs. Slots should be about 1/8" deep maximum. Apply epoxy to the wrapped hook shank and in the slots in the body. Insert the hook and rubber hackle legs into their respective slots, align the hook and body and allow the epoxy to harden.

8. Slice a thin piece of foam for the fly's belly. Try to use a slice with the adhesive coated surface on one side. Press the foam slice into place to form the belly of the fly. Trim the edges even with the body, being **very careful not to cut off the rubber hackle legs**. Trim body to final shape at this time. Trim legs to desired length.

9. Use waterproof felt marking pens to color the body. Both markings and colors are optional, however, the belly of the bug should be white or a light color, the top and sides darker.

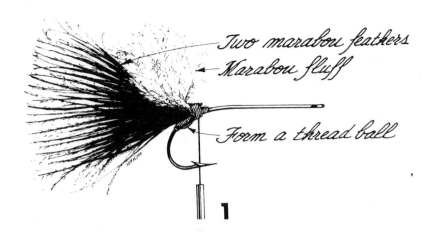

Two marabou feathers
Marabou fluff
Form a thread ball

1

Materials:

Hook: Size 1 Mustad-Sproat #3366 RE Bronzed or #3399 TDE Bronzed

Thread: Size "A" Nylon — Black

Tail: (Tie in order) Two Marabou Feathers — Marabou Fluff (barbs) of contrasting color — Four Webby Hen Hackles — One Large Rooster Neck Hackle

Butt: Medium Diameter Chenille

Body: Deer Body Hair, Medium Sized, 3-4 dyed colors spun in bands

Legs: Medium Rubber Hackle

Head: None

Cements: Vinyl for tying — Ambroid Model Cement for facial rigidity

Face: Black Lacquer

PATTERN NO. 21

Stoner's Bass Bug

Type: Popping Bug, spun hair type

Simulates: Large terrestrial insect

Habitat: Freshwater rivers, lakes, ponds

Takes: Large and Smallmouth Bass, panfish

Background: While Larry Stoner, of Costa Mesa, California, cannot take credit for constructing popping bug bodies from spun deer body hair, he has elevated the technique to an art form. Indeed, Larry is a professional artist and all of the flies from his vise reflect his talent. The selection of materials and colors, and his detailing of this popping bug pattern are especially handsome. What's more, the bass all seem to agree, and when it's tied small enough, so do the bluegill. Larry's principal innovation, and which in large measure accounts for the fly's pronounced "**Pop**" sound when it's being retrieved, is his use of ambroid model cement to give the bug's "face" rigidity and durability.

Color is your choice. Duplicate the two examples shown in this book or invent your own scheme. How it's tied is what's important.

1. Leave the entire shank bare. Start the fly just past the bend and form a ⅛" diameter thread ball approximately ⅓ down the bend. Cement. Tie two hook length marabou feathers atop the hook eyeward of the thread ball. The feathers should be paired and tied in to extend horizontally with their flat sides vertical. Tie a small clump of marabou fluff atop the feather butts. Wrap securely in place.

2. Trim four hen hackles to hook length. Match and cement them in pairs at their butts. Tie one pair on each side of the marabou feathers, concave sides outward, tips pointing slightly downward. Trim off the excess butts. Tie in a large rooster neck hackle atop the butts. Trim off the excess butt.

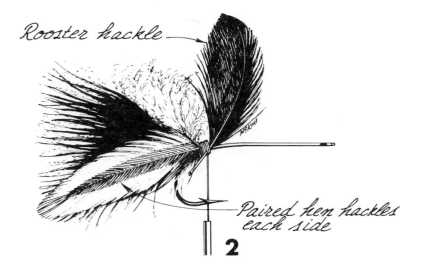

Rooster hackle

Paired hen hackles
each side

2

3. Spin the rooster hackle 5 or 6 turns in place, tie off
and trim the excess tip. Cement. Tie in a 3-inch
length of chenille, make 2 wraps to form a butt,
then tie off and trim the excess chenille.
Half-hitch and cement. The front of the butt
should be even with the hook's point — the shank
bare metal.

4. Trim off the hair tips from a piece of deer body
hide, leaving the attached hairs 1¼ inches long.
Trim off a ¼ inch clump and brush out the
underhairs. Tie the hairs on the bare hook shank
with two wraps of thread at mid-clump. Start
tightening the wraps during the second wrap.
Release your grip and allow the hairs to flare,
separate and slide around the hook. Take a third
wrap around the first two then work the thread
thru the spun hairs and take two wraps in front.
Half-hitch. Use your fingers or a packing tool to
jam the hairs against the chenille butt. Cement
the connection.

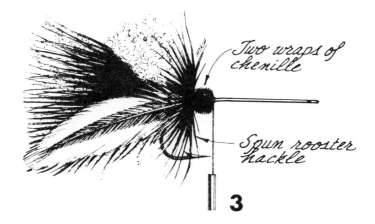

Two wraps of
chenille

Spun rooster
hackle

3

Clump of spun deer body hair

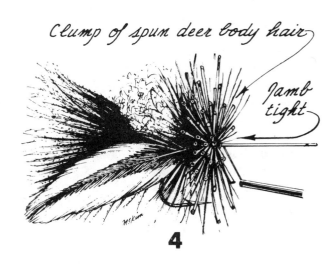

Jamb
tight

4

(Continued next page)

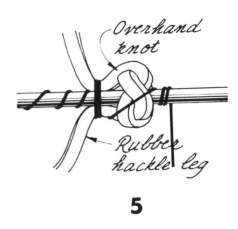

Overhand knot

Rubber hackle leg

5

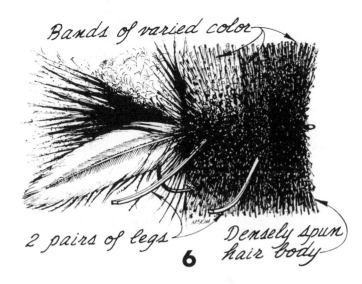

Bands of varied color

2 pairs of legs

Densely spun hair body

6

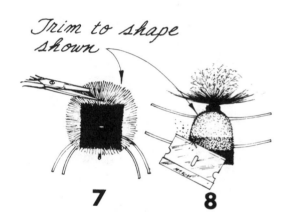

Trim to shape shown

7   **8**

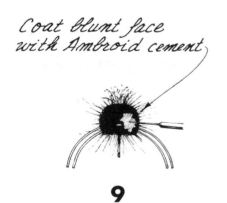

Coat blunt face with Ambroid cement

9

5. Tie a loose overhand knot in the center of a 3-inch length of rubber hackle and slip the knot over the eye of the hook. Tighten the knot and pull the two ends parallel to the shank. Take two thread wraps behind the knot, then two in front. Push the knot against the spun deer hair, gently pull the legs perpendicular to the shank and liberally cement the leg in place.

6. Continue spinning and packing the hair body. Spin bands of different, graduated colors — light in back, dark at eye. Cement each clump. Add another pair of legs ¼ inch from the eye. Whip finish at the eye, clip off the thread and cement the connection.

7. You're now ready to trim the body of the fly. Facing the eye, use scissors to trim the body to a square shape. **Be very careful not to cut off the legs and hackle!**

8. With a sharp razor blade or scissors trim to the body shape shown — flat on the underside — rounded on the sides, top and rear — flat on the face. The finished body should be a densely packed mass. Trim the rubber hackle legs equally on both sides.

9. After the trimming is complete, coat the face with Ambroid Model Cement and let thoroughly dry. Lightly paint the face with black lacquer to impart shine. Thoroughly impregnate the body with a high quality moisture repellent liquid or spray and let the fly dry overnight.

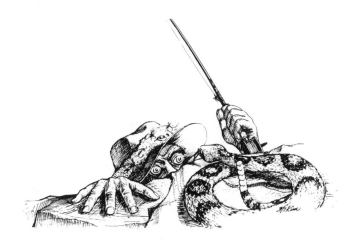

The Challenge

I've chosen to leave the next three patterns for last. To have presented them within their respective categories would have been both untimely and unfair. They are not the easiest flies to tie. Having reached this point in your development as a tier of flies, none of the three should offer more than an interesting challenge... and, I hope... an adventure in fur, feathers and foam.

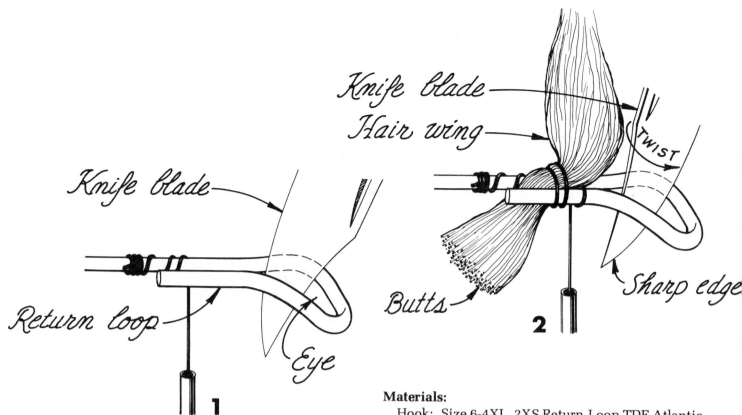

PATTERN NO. 22
Salmon Black

Type: Wet Fly, Steelhead "Attractor" Type

Simulates: (Probably) baitfish

Habitat: Freshwater rivers

Takes: Steelhead Trout

Background: This is one of the patterns tied by Edward L. Haas, Forks of Salmon, California, a professional tier and inveterate "steelie" fisherman. With his permission (Ed's loath to name his flies) I've named the fly after his home river, a tributary of the Klamath, plus the fly's general coloration. Ed always ties his flies on return-loop hooks, using his unique method of tying in the hair wing. Combined with meticulous attention to each detail of the fly's construction (he's the most exacting perfectionist I know) the result is a fly so durable and beautiful you hate to get it wet. In the event that you cannot obtain, or do not wish to tie this fly on the loop hook shown, substitute a standard steelhead hook and tie the wing in to suit.

Materials:

Hook: Size 6-4XL, 2XS Return-Loop TDE Atlantic Salmon Hook

Thread: Size 3/0 or 6/0 Danville's Flymaster or equal — Black

Wing: Natural Black Squirrel — extremely soft

Aft Body: Red Floss

Rib: Silver Mylar, small or small Silver Tinsel

Body: Black Chenille

Hackle: Black, wet

Head: Tying Thread

Cement: Cellire Varnish (Veniard's) or substitute for head only

1. Tie in the thread behind the hook's return loop. Pry open the eye with a knife and slip two thread wraps between the loop return and shank.

2. Trim a clump of squirrel hairs, even up the tips and tie the butts atop the shank, tips toward the eye. Start with 2 loose wraps, then gently pry the eye open with the knife point and work the butts down between shank and loop return. Lift the wing hairs to the vertical position and take one thread wrap in front.

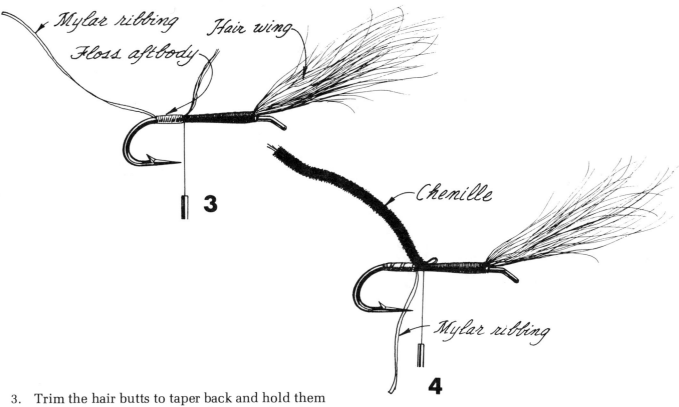

Mylar ribbing Hair wing

Floss aftbody

3

Chenille

Mylar ribbing

4

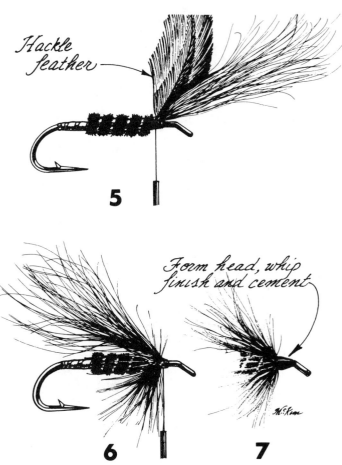

Hackle feather

5

Form head, whip finish and cement

6   **7**

3. Trim the hair butts to taper back and hold them alongside the shank. Bring the tying thread behind the wing and wrap to the hook's bend with tight consecutive turns. Tie in the ribbing material, then floss. Wrap the floss aft body, tie off and trim the excess floss.

4. Take one complete turn with ribbing at the tail, then rib the aft body. Tie off but **do not** trim the excess ribbing. Coat the aft body with varnish or cement and let dry. Tie in chenille and bring the tying thread forward to the wing.

5. Coat the shank with cement and wrap a chenille body. Tie off the chenille 1/16 inch behind the wing and trim the excess. Rib the chenille body with the remaining ribbing material, tie off and trim the excess. Tie in the hackle feather.

6. Spin the entire hackle, then secure it in place by working the thread back and forth between the spun barbs, finishing at the wing. Trim off the excess hackle tip. Lift the wing and wrap the thread in front of the wing, forcing the wing hairs to lay back.

7. Form a tapering head, smaller toward the eye. Hackle fibers should extend straight down. Whip finish and clip the tying thread. Coat the head with varnish or head cement.

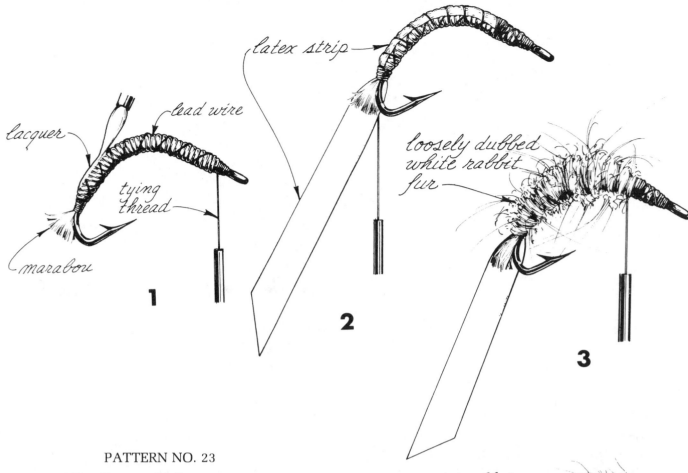

lacquer

lead wire

latex strip

tying thread

marabou

1

2

loosely dubbed white rabbit fur

3

PATTERN NO. 23

Gilled Caddis Larva

Type: Nymph Type Wet Fly

Simulates: Larval stage of the Caddisfly (order *Trichoptera*)

Habitat: Freshwater rivers and streams, lakes

Takes: Trout

Background: This pattern was originated by Wayne Luallen, a gifted young professional fly tier from Visalia, California. While it may be more involved and perhaps difficult for the beginner to tie, we have included the fly because it introduces a versatile material — latex — and has enjoyed marked success on the stream. Caddis are found nearly everywhere in great abundance and form a significant portion of the trout's diet. Caddis, like mayflies, come in many color schemes depending upon species. Choose colors to match the local variety, tie to match the fly shown in this book, or make the thorax dark brown, the abdomen light cream or white.

expose rabbit hairs to form abdominal gills

spirally wrap latex to form abdomen

4

Materials:

Hook: Sizes 12-14 Mustad #37140, or 16-18 Mustad #37160 RE Bronzed

Thread: Size 6/0 to 8/0 Flymaster Prewaxed — color to match thorax

Anal Prolegs (or Gills): Marabou Barbs — color to match insect

Underbody: Lead Wire wrapped under dubbed white rabbit fur

Abdomen: Strip of Latex Sheet Rubber

Thorax: Dubbed Fur of appropriate color

Legs: Ringneck Pheasant Center Tail Feather Barbs — knotted

Head: Tying Thread

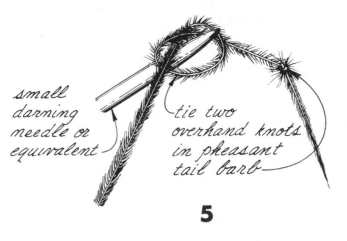

small darning needle or equivalent

tie two overhand knots in pheasant tail barb

5

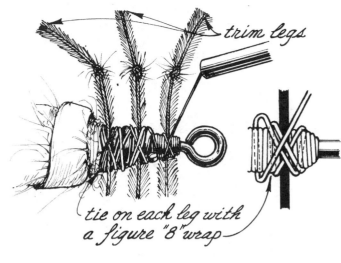

trim legs

tie on each leg with a figure "8" wrap

6

1. Start at the eye and wrap consecutive turns to the position on the shank shown. Tie in a stubby fluff of marabou. This represents either anal gills of *Hydropsyche* caddis or the prolegs of *Rhyacophila* caddis. Wrap lead wire solidly along the hook's shank, secure with a few spiraled wraps of thread and coat with lacquer or head cement. Wraps should end at the eye.

2. Trim a strip of latex at an angle and tie its tip in at the start of the thorax. Stretch the latex back atop the lead underbody and tie it down in front of the marabou. This will make a smooth underbody.

3. Twist white rabbit fur on the tying thread and form a **loosely** dubbed body. Wrap to the thorax.

4. Now wrap the latex strip snugly toward the thorax, lapping each succeeding joint. Do not wrap too tightly or the body will lose its segmented effect. As you wrap, allow some of the rabbit hairs to extend backward between the latex layers to act as abdominal gills.

5. Select three similar barbs from a pheasant tail feather and tie two overhand knots in each. Try to tie the knots in each of the three barbs equidistant. Trim the barbs to form the fly's three pairs of legs.

6. With the fly upside down in the vise, tie each "set" of legs individually in place with figure "8" wraps of thread.

7. Build the thorax with dubbed rabbit fur of an appropriate color, wrapping between the three sets of legs.

8. Form a small tying thread head and whip finish. Clip thread and coat the entire thorax and head with lacquer. This secures the head and legs and imparts the sheen to the back of the thorax seen on the live insect. After the lacquer has dried, use a permanent felt marker of an appropriate color to mark the abdomen as follows: **toward** the **eye** on the **sides** and **back**; **toward** the **bend** on the **underside** of the fly's body. This method allows the ink to flow into the joints on the side and back and emphasizes the segmented appearance of the live caddis larva. The marker dyes the white rabbit hairs at the same time.

dub thorax between each pair of legs

legs

7

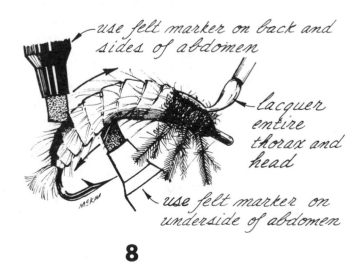

use felt marker on back and sides of abdomen

lacquer entire thorax and head

use felt marker on underside of abdomen

8

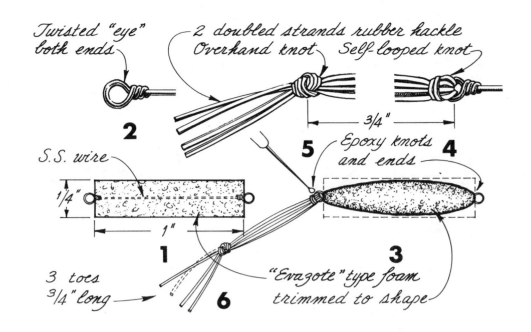

Twisted "eye" both ends

2 doubled strands rubber hackle
Overhand knot   **Self-looped knot**

2

S.S. wire

1/4"

1"

1

5

3/4"

Epoxy knots and ends

4

3

3 toes 3/4" long →

6

"Evazote" type foam trimmed to shape

PATTERN NO. 24

McKim's Evafloat'n Frog

Type: Surface Popping Bug

Simulates: Frog

Habitat: Freshwater lakes, ponds, sloughs

Takes: Largemouth Bass

Background: Except for the material from which the body and hindlegs are constructed, there's nothing really new about this pattern. Even the wiggle-leg concept is an idea I borrowed from the famous and talented writer and fly tier, Dave Whitlock. But where frog popper bodies have been variously constructed of materials ranging from cork, balsa and other materials including spun deer body hair, insofar as I am able to determine, I am the first to employ "Evazote" closed cell foam for buoyancy. In my opinion, "Evazote" is the most nearly perfect material being produced for the purpose. It possesses superior buoyancy, floats indefinitely, is both compressible and resilient and offers excellent durability. It is easy to work, heat bondable to itself, or with epoxy, and can be colored with waterproof markers. It also comes in a range of colors and white. Closed cell polyethylene foams perform nearly as well, and both "Evazote" or a suitable closed cell polyethylene foam can be substituted where the pattern calls for a cork type body. I believe the potential uses for both "Evazote" and closed cell polyethylene foams in fly tying are virtually unexplored.

Materials:

Hook: Size 1, XL Mustad #33903 Kink-Shank, RE, Bronzed

Thread: Size "A" Nylon — White

Weedguard: 30 to 40# test Monofilament Fishing Line

Structural Hinge: Fine Stainless Steel Wire

Hindlegs: Thighs — "Evazote" or closed-cell Polyethylene Foam
Calves/Toes — Medium Rubber Hackle

Body: "Evazote" or closed-cell Polyethylene Foam

Forelegs: Medium Rubber Hackle

Eyes: Plastic Beads

Cement: Clear 2-part 5-minute Epoxy

Finishes: Pantone-type Waterproof Markers — Clear Acrylic Spray

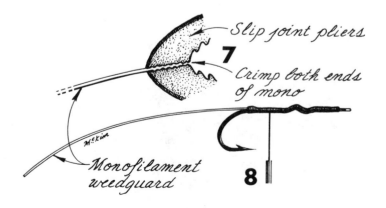

Slip joint pliers

7

Crimp both ends of mono

McKim

Monofilament weedguard

8

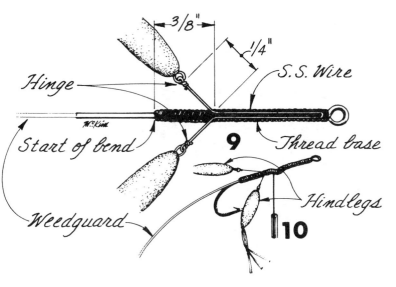

Hindlegs

1. Slice off two strips of foam ¼" square x 1-inch long for thighs.

2. Cut two 2-inch lengths of stainless steel wire and use pliers to twist a ⅛" diameter loop "eye" in one end of each wire. Force the straight ends lengthwise thru the foam strips. Place the "eyed" end in your tying vise and, compressing the foam against the vise, form a second loop "eye" at the opposite end of the thigh. When finished, the "eyes" should just protrude from each end of the thigh.

3. Use scissors to shape both thighs to match.

4. To form the calves and toes, double two strands of rubber hackle and insert the loops through the "eye" at the narrow end of the thigh. Thread the loose ends through the rubber loops. Tighten the self-loop connection.

5. Tie an overhand knot in the four strands of rubber hackle about ¾-inch from the thigh.

6. Trim the free ends to make three ¾-inch toes. Epoxy the knots and thigh ends. Leave "eye" clear.

Weedguard

7. Cut a length of monofilament long enough to loosely reach around the bend to the hook's eye. Crimp both ends with slip-joint toothed pliers.

8. Start back of the eye and wrap tying thread closely to the bend. Tie the mono atop the shank at the bend. Allow the other end to hang freely. Advance the thread ⅜" forward of the bend.

Hinges

9. Pass one end of a length of wire through the thigh's open "eye" and twist to form a loose looped connection. Allow 2-inches between the legs and repeat the procedure with the opposite thigh. These form the legs' hinges. Bend the wire double at its mid-point, then at opposing 45 degree angles about ¼-inch from each thigh.

10. Tie the bent hinge wire atop the shank, legs toward the rear. Hinge wires should start to diverge from the shank ⅜-inch forward of the bend. Advance thread to mid-shank.

Forelegs

11. Using 3 strands of rubber hackle, tie 2 overhand knots 2-inches apart.

12. Center the hackle forelegs and figure "8" wrap into place atop mid-shank. Trim both ends to form three ¾-inch fingers.

13. Lift the mono weedguard and secure below the shank behind the eye. Allow at least ⅛-inch clearance below the point. Whip finish, clip thread and cement.

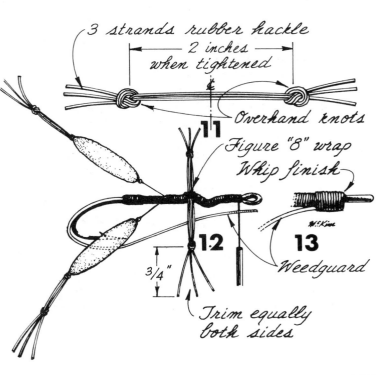

127

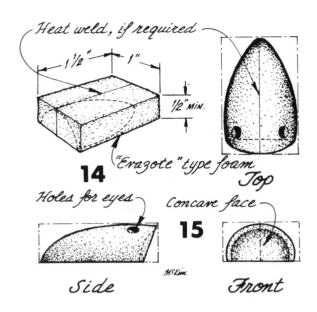

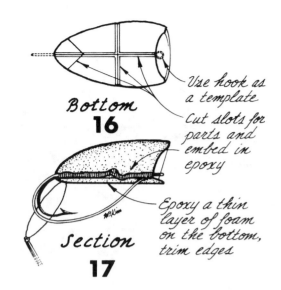

Body

14. If your foam is one piece, 1''x½''x1½'', simply trim to shape. If not, heat weld two or more smaller pieces together by pressing the flat surfaces of two pieces against a moderately warm electric iron, then against each other. The pieces will permanently bond. Use this process to form a layered block of foam larger than the body of the frog.

15. With scissors or a sharp razor blade trim the body to shape. Cut two holes in the top to receive plastic beads for eyes. After shaping, press the blunt face, and top and bottom surfaces briefly on a warm iron to smooth and seal the body's surface. **Be careful!** Overheating will melt the foam.

16. Using the incomplete fly as a template, cut slots in the bottom sufficiently deep to completely embed the shank, hinge wires and forelegs. The hook's eye should nestle in the concave face — the hindleg hinges close against the sides.

17. Coat the thread-wrapped shank and fill all body slots with epoxy. Press the body into position, fully embedding all parts. Cut a thin layer of foam to cover the bottom of the body. Epoxy into place and trim the edges smooth when dry. Epoxy plastic bead eyes in place.

Coloring

18. With waterproof markers, color the body and other parts as shown. When thoroughly dried, spray all foam surfaces with clear acrylic.

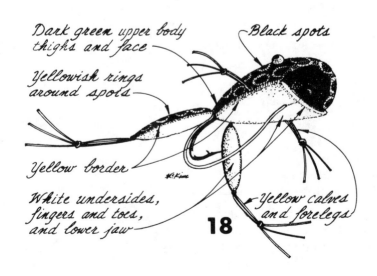

Glossary

Adams. Fly pattern; also mixed grizzly and brown hackles.

Aft Body. See Body.

Angora. Angora rabbit fur; made as soft yarn, dyed in colors.

Attractor. Any fly pattern not designed to imitate a specific insect or other natural living baitform, relying solely on form, flash or other distinctive qualities to attract fish.

Barb. 1. Part of a feather (see Feather). 2. On a hook, the backward projecting point meant to prevent easy extraction.

Barbicel. A part of a feather (see Feather).

Barbule. A part of a feather (see Feather).

Bead Chain. All metal flexible cord of small strung beads; cut in pairs and tied to simulate buggy eyes on a fly.

Beard. Small clump of hackle barbs tied below the hook's shank extending back from behind the fly's head.

Bend. On a hook, the curved portion connecting the shank and barbed or pointed projection.

Bobbin. Hand held tool used for controlled thread supply.

Bodkin. Tool for applying cement, wax, for cleaning the eye and other purposes; syn. *dubbing needle*.

Body. Main portion of fly constructed on or around hook between the tail and head; simulates bodies of living baitforms; fore and aft bodies are portions extending before or behind the center joint. Insect bodies are divided into three parts as follows:

> **Head.** Front segment; contains eyes and mouth.
> **Thorax.** Middle segment; includes nymphal wingpads; supports legs and wings.
> **Abdomen.** Rear segment; contains stomach and digestive organs; in ants, the *gaster*.

Breast. Of birds, front of the body below the neck; a type of feather from the same area of the body.

Bucktail. 1. Type of fly, usually a baitfish imitation, with a hair back and/or wing. 2. Tail hair from members of the deer family.

Butt. 1. On a fly, the small ring of material between body and tail. 2. The thickest part of the feather's quill nearest the bird's body.

Caddis or Caddisfly. Aquatic insect (order *Trichoptera*), tailless; three phases — larva, pupa, (tent winged) adult.

Center Joint. A ring of material similar to the butt, midway on shank.

Chamois. A soft, pliant leather made of antelope, sheep, goat.

Cheek. On a fly, a larger feather than the shoulder; tied behind the shoulder if both are used.

Chenille. A soft, fluffy cord having a fuzzy pile on all sides, made from various natural and synthetic fibers twisted between a two-stranded core. (French: *caterpillar*.)

Collar. A ring of material between body and wing (or hackle); in the typical Shad Fly pattern the collar occurs between hackle and eyes.

Contour. The types of feathers which cover the body and collectively give the bird its distinctive shape.

Cree. Tan chicken feather, laterally barred brownish-black, similar to grizzly.

Deer Hair. Hair of the deer family; usually refers to deer body hair, as differentiated from bucktail (tail hairs); a soft, compressible (erroneously termed "hollow") fiber extensively used in fly tying.

Down. The fluffy barbs near the butt of a feather; also a type of feather next to the body not used to tie flies.

Downwing. A type of fly wing (see Wing).

Dressing. The act of applying materials to a hook to construct a fly; also the materials except the hook which comprise the finished fly; syn. *tying the fly*.

Dry Fly. Type of fly designed to float, usually an insect or spider imitation; simulates freshly emerged or dead or dying adult floating on the water's surface.

Dry Hackle. Hackle with greatly reduced barbules, stiff barbs, minimum "web" area.

Dubbing. Fur or similar soft fibers intended for body material; also, the technique of twisting such material with the tying thread to form a furry strand of body material.

Dubbing Needle. Syn. *bodkin.*

Dubbing Wax. Special tacky wax used to adhere dubbing material to the tying thread.

Dun. 1. First stage of the adult mayfly. 2. Any soft, dull greyish color.

Egg-sack. A (fly) butt used to simulate the egg-sack of an insect.

Emerger. Type of fly with nymphal shape and stubby downwings; imitates mayfly hatched underwater swimming to surface.

Epoxy. Type of two-part adhesive; hardens when mixed in correct proportions; clear type is used to bond and coat fly parts.

Evazote. Trade mark of Bakelite Xylonite Limited for its closed cell foamed cross-linked ethylene vinyl acetate product; an extremely buoyant foam with great fly tying potential.

Eye. 1. Part of hook where line is connected. 2. A small feather tied to simulate a baitfish eye on streamer and bucktail fly patterns (syn. *shoulder*). 3. Anything, painted or tied, intended to simulate the eye of a baitfish, insect or other living creature. 4. Distinctive "eye" pattern forming the tip of peacock tail feathers.

Feather. The body covering and wing flight surface element of birds; includes different types designed to perform a variety of specific functions; not all feathers are suited to fly tying; feathers used to tie flies include hackle, primary and secondary, breast, flank, tail, ornamental plumage and a few others except down. Most feathers are obtained from wildfowl such as gamecocks, waterfowl, pheasant species and others; while the size, shape and frequency of each part varys among the different kinds of feathers, all feathers have at least three of the following structural elements in common:

> **Quill** (or **stem**). The main central shaft, the butt of which is imbedded in the bird.
>
> **Barb** (or **fiber**). Lateral fiber branching from both sides of the quill, individually distinct on hackles.
>
> **Barbule.** Lateral fiber branching from one or both sides of a barb, collectively referred to as the "web."
>
> **Barbicel.** Projection, often hook-tipped, present on the barbules of some types of feathers; mechanically binds the barbs together (nature's "zipper").

Figure-8. Wrapping technique; separates and secures the fly's parts.

Fiber. Threadlike component of a substance; syn. (feather) *barb.*

Flank. On birds, the areas below the wing along each side; also the contour feathers that cover the bird's flanks.

Flight. A type of wing feather; syn. *secondary.*

Floss. A lustrous 1 to 4 strand flat yarn made from silk, rayon, nylon and other fibers, available in many colors including radiantly dyed types; untwisted glossy yarn made for tying flies.

Fluff. Syn. *down.*

Fly. 1. A fishhook dressed with suitable materials intended to deceive and catch fish; an artificial lure the weight of which is nonessential to the act of casting, as opposed to a weighted lure such as a leadhead jig; paradoxically, added weight is desirable when presenting deeply fished flies such as nymphs. 2. A type of living insect.

Fur. General term for the soft, dense hairy growth covering the bodies of so-called fur bearing mammals; includes both the *underfur* and *guard hairs.*

Gap. The space separating the point from the shank of a hook measured at its closest proximity.

Golden Pheasant Crest. Slim, stiff feathers from the top of the head of the Golden Pheasant that resemble metallic gold strands.

Grizzly. Feather from Plymouth Rock breed of chicken; grey to near white background, laterally barred dark grey to black; syn. *Barred Rock.*

Guard Hair. Type of body hair; collectively, the stiff lustrous hairs that extend above the underfur on fur bearing mammals.

Guinea Fowl. A type of bird; also the bird's dark, slaty, white speckled plumage; syn. *Guinea Hen.*

Hackle. 1. A fly part; feather, hair or other fibers tied so as to radiate from the bodies of certain flies (see Spun and Palmer). 2. Types of contour feathers lacking barbicels found principally on the neck and back of the bird; rooster (chicken) hackles are of the following types:

> **Neck.** Narrow; relatively stiff quill and barbs; found covering the entire neck and back of the head.
> **Spade.** Short; wide; relatively stiff quill and barbs; found on upper back and shoulder of wings; also called *shoulder hackles.*
> **Saddle.** Long; slim; limber quill; stiff shiny barbs; found on the back between spade hackles and tail.
> **Spey.** Long; relatively wide; limber quill; "webby" barbs; found on the sides of the tail near its base.

Hackle Pliers. Tool used to grasp the hackle's tip during the tying process.

Hair. The threadlike fibers that grow from the skin of mammals; in fur bearing mammals, both the underfur and guard hairs.

Hair Tamper. Tool used to align the tips of deer body hairs and bucktail; syn. *hair stacker.*

Half-hitch. A type of knot used to secure materials during the tying process, sometimes used to finish the fly.

Head. 1. Usually the last fly part completed behind the eye of the hook. 2. Front segment of an insect's body and the body part of living baitforms containing eyes and mouth.

Head Cement. Specially formulated clear liquid adhesive used to coat the head of the finished fly, and for bonding fly parts during the tying process.

Herl. The long, limber "feathery" barbs on peacock tail feathers, ostrich plumes, etc.

Hook. 1. A fishhook; a device, usually of wire, forged or unforged, designed and shaped to catch fish; consists of the following parts: eye, shank, bend, barb (if any) and point. 2. Fly part upon which materials are dressed.

Horns. A fly part; single pair of feather barbs (not sections) tied on at the head, extending over the wings or topping.

Jamb Knot. Technique of binding the tying thread to the shank by a series of overlying wraps of thread; used to start the tying process.

Kip. Cow tail hair; natural or dyed colors; syn. *impali.*

Larva. The immature, wormlike pre-pupa stage of certain insects including caddis flies; larva are distinguished from nymphs by the absence of wing pads.

Latex. Very thin, flexible, so-called "live" rubber (also called "dental dam"); comes in natural or dyed colors.

Lead Wire. Small buss fuse wire used to weight fly bodies; comes in three diameters.

Marabou. Very soft, downy barbed, limber quilled feather; wing and tail feathers of the marabou stork (some "marabou" is from the turkey).

May Fly. Also **mayfly**; aquatic insect (order *Ephemeroptera*), tailed; three forms: **nymph**, (unwinged) **dun** and **spinner** adults; numerous fly patterns imitate each form.

Mohair. Type of yarn; hair of the Angora goat.

Mosquito. Aquatic insect (order *Diptera*), tailless; three forms: **larva, pupa, adult**; flies usually imitate adult form.

Mylar. 1. A metalized gold or silver thin, narrow plastic ribbon, also made in colors; also called **mylar tinsel**. 2. A transparent plastic.

Mylar Tubing. Metalized mylar braided to enclose a cotton stranded core; with core removed, the mylar tube is used as fly body material; imitates the body scales of baitfish; also called **mylar piping**.

Neck. The neck skin of a chicken with hackles still attached; syn. *cape*; neck consists of two parts:

> **Nape.** Smaller section equals hackles size 18 and smaller.
> **Butt.** Larger section equals hackles size 16 and larger.

Noodle. Fur rolled to a round slender length for use as dubbing.

Nymo. Type of flat stranded nylon thread no longer made.

Nymph. 1. Any immature two-phase, tailed aquatic insect with wing pads, such as a pre-dun phase mayfly. 2. A type of fly that imitates an insect's nymphal phase.

Overbody. The exposed finished body farthest from the hook's point.

Overwing. Uppermost part of the wing when the wing has two or more parts.

Padding. Any material applied under another to fill out or shape any part of a fly.

Palmer. Tying technique; hackle wrapped spirally along a length, as along the body of a fly; hackle so wrapped is called **palmered hackle,** the process **palmering.**

Parachute. Hackle spun horizontally around a vertical support arising from the shank, such as an upright wing or other projection. Some hooks include a built-in support for spinning parachute hackle.

Pattern. 1. Fly — a standardized model; similar or identical materials tied in established relationships to form a distinct silhouette. 2. Hook — a series proportionately identical, differing in relative sizes; syn. *style.*

Peacock Eye. Distinctively "eyed" tip of peacock's tail plumage.

Peacock Sword. Type of ornamental plumage on the peacock (bird).

Pointer. Type of flight feather; one of the first six feathers on the tip of the bird's wings; syn. *primary.*

Polyethylene Foam. Closed-cell plastic foam; suitable for popper and other floating fly bodies; extremely light and buoyant.

Polypropylene. Synthetic fiber; extremely water repellent material; used as dubbing material, fly wing material; range of colors; available as yarn and loose dubbing material.

Popper. Type of floating fly with a body made of cork, spun deer body hair, plastic foam or other material; designed usually to make a "popping" sound when vigorously retrieved across the water's surface.

Primary. A pointed, smooth surfaced vane-like wing feather; syn. *pointer.*

Quill. 1. The central hollow shaft of a feather; syn. *stem.* 2. A section of attached barbs trimmed from primary or similar vane-like feathers for use as a fly wing, such as a **quill wing.**

Raffia. Fiber from the raffia palm tree (natural or dyed colors).

Rib, Ribbing. 1. Any thread or threadlike material wrapped spirally along the fly's body. 2. Tying technique to form the rib.

Rubber Hackle. Fiber-like, soft "live" rubber used for legs on certain types of flies, notably popping bugs.

Saddle. A type of hackle feather (see Feather); also a section of the bird's back skin with the hackles attached.

Sash. Portion of fly body between collar and butt, usually made of bright material.

Scud. Any of various amphipod crustaceans, commonly but mistakenly known as "freshwater shrimp"; a fly pattern.

Secondary. A blunt-tipped vane-surfaced feather from the wing's trailing edge near the body of the bird; usually, ten feathers on each wing; syn. *flight.*

Shank. Of a hook; portion between the eye and the bend.

Shellcase. The crustlike shell covering the back and sides of crustaceans such as shrimp, scud, sandcrabs and similar living species; materials used to simulate these shells include plastics, latex, swisstraw, hair, etc.

Shoulder. A fly part; small feather on the side intended to simulate the eye of a baitfish; not *shoulder* (spade) hackle.

Spent. 1. A type of fly wing (see Wing). 2. A dead or dying insect.

Spin. Tying technique; act of spinning a material around the shank or body of the fly.

Spinner. Final winged stage in the life of a mayfly.

Splayed. Two parts with diverging tips, such as tail fibers and wings that spread apart as they leave the body (see Wings).

Split Bead. Small hollow brass bead cut nearly in two; used for head or other fly body parts.

Spun. Any multi-fibered material spun around the hook so that its individual fibers flare or radiate from the shank or body of the fly; spun deer body hair is applied in small bunches; **spun hackle** refers to the feather wrapped in one small area (see Palmer and Hackle).

Stem. Syn. *quill.*

Stonefly. Aquatic insect (order *Plecoptera*), tailed; two phases: **nymph** and (folded wing) **adult.**

Streamer. Type of fly; usually a baitfish imitation with a feather back and/or wing; see (Bucktail).

Strips. A fly part; matched pair of primary type barb sections, usually long and slender, placed near the top edge or in the center of the wing.

Style. Syn. *pattern*.

Swisstraw. A single-stranded viscose rayon ribbon which flattens when wetted; available in over 40 different colors.

Tag. A band of tinsel, mylar, floss, or other material on the shank under the tail.

Tail. A fly part, usually the rearmost projection from the shank of the hook.

Tail Tag. A very short stubby tail, usually wool or floss.

Terrestrial. Type of fly; simulates various forms of land-oriented insects such as ants, caterpillars, spiders, etc.

Tinsel. An all-metal silver or gold plated, flat, oval, smooth or embossed strand, available in several widths (see Mylar).

Tip. 1. Fly — band of tinsel, mylar, floss on the shank directly behind the body and encircling the tail. 2. Feather — small end opposite the butt of the quill.

Tippet. 1. Neck hackles of the pheasant. 2. The tip section of a fly line leader; specifically the end that connects to the tied fly.

Topping. Herl or similar long, usually bright colored material tied atop the overwing of a streamer or bucktail fly.

Trailers. Matched feather sections such as short pheasant crest, one above and the other below the body, tied on at the center joint.

Turkey. A large bird; also the wing, tail and other feathers of the turkey that are used to tie flies.

Tying Thread. Also termed **tying silk**; the continuous filament, usually multi-stranded fiber, used to bind the parts of a fly together; made of nylon or silk in various colors and sizes.

Underbody. The exposed finished body part closest to the hook point.

Underfur. The soft hairs that densely cover the bodies of fur bearing mammals; (see Guard Hair).

Underwing. The underpart of the wing when the wing has two parts.

Upwing. Type of fly wing; (see Wing).

Vise. A tool designed to hold the hook firmly in position during the process of tying the fly.

Wax. Special non-drying tacky compounds made for fly tying; usually formulated in three grades: No. 1, **thread coating**; No's 2 and 3, **dubbing.**

Web. 1. Numerous and pronounced barbules lacking barbicels. 2. In hackle, the distinct triangular areas seen on both sides of the quill, widest near the butt of the feather and tapering toward its tip.

Wet Fly. Type of fly; generally, any fly (usually an insect imitation) dressed sparsely so as to quickly sink; a sinking pattern intended to be fished below the surface.

Wet Hackle. Hackle whose barbs contain numerous and pronounced overlapping barbules; a heavily "webbed" feather; hen chicken hackle is an example of totally "webby" wet type hackle (see Dry Hackle).

Whip Finish. A type of knot used to complete the fly; may be tied with either special whip-finishing tools or by the so-called "two hand whip finish" tying technique; a knot that results in a flat lay of thread without bulges.

Wing. 1. The flight sustaining appendage of birds, insects and other flying creatures or devices. 2. The fly part meant to imitate the wings of insects or (in the case of streamer type flies) the upper portion of the body and tail of baitfish; fly wings are made from a variety of materials including feathers, hair, plastic films and other natural and synthetic fibers; with respect to a hook as viewed from its side, the three basic types of fly wings and their orientation are: **down** (horizontal, parallel to the shank), **up** (vertical, perpendicular to the shank) and **spent** (horizontal, perpendicular to the shank, tips opposed); (see Appendix Plate 4, Typical Fly Wing Types).

Wingcase. Syn. *wing pads*.

Wing Pads. The hard case over the thorax of a nymph covering its folded wings.

Wrap. A turn of a material around the axial shaft of the hook, usually of thread or another strand-type product, made to secure a part of the fly; also the act of wrapping, as to *wrap the body*.

Yarn. A twisted strand made from natural or synthetic fibers or a combination of both types.

Yarn Tye. A thick, loosely twisted gift wrapping cord made from acrylic fibers, available in a range of bright colors.

Sources

In addition to my own ideas and experiences, much of the practical know-how in this book is a reflection of the shared thoughts of fellow tiers. Some of these ideas may be appearing here for the first time in print. If true, I am all the more indebted to those individuals.

A number of written sources — unpublished and published — were also consulted in order to establish a firm factual basis for the assertions made herein. By "unpublished" I mean written material printed and distributed on such a limited scale that, for all intents and purposes, it must be considered unavailable to you, the reader. This includes material such as club newsletters and fly tying class instructional literature. "Published" works, on the other hand, includes both books and the catalogs of manufacturers, distributors and dealers. Books on fly tying can usually be purchased or borrowed from a local library. Catalogs may be obtained free or at a nominal charge by writing to the appropriate source.

It is not my intent to list all of the sources of materials and literature on the subject; others, notably Terry Helleckson in his excellent book *Popular Fly Patterns*, have already done a thorough job in this vein. But I most enthusiastically seize this opportunity to recommend the sources I found helpful in writing this book. In the pursuit of knowledge, exposure to differing points of view is always of value.

Books & Periodicals

Bates, J.D. *Streamer Fly Tying & Fishing.* Stackpole Books, 1976

Bay, K.E. *How To Tie Freshwater Flies.* Winchester Press, 1976

Bay, K.E. *Salt Water Flies.* Lippincott, 1972

Bay, K.E. *The American Fly Tyer's Handbook.* Winchester Press, 1979

Boyle, R.H. & Whitlock, D. *The Fly Tyer's Almanac.* Crown Publishers, Inc., 1975

Caucci, A. & Nastasi, B. *Hatches.* Comparahatch Ltd., 1975

FFF BULLETIN *The Tie Flyer.* Quarterly publication for members. The Federation of Fly Fishermen, West Yellowstone, Montana

Flick, A. *Art Flick's Master Fly Tying Guide.* Crown Publishers, Inc., 1972

Fulsher, K. *Tying and Fishing the Thunder Creek Series.* Freshet Press, Inc., 1973

Helleckson, T. *Popular Fly Patterns.* Peregrine Smith, Inc., 1977

Herter, G.L. *Professional Fly Tying and Tackle Making Manual and Manufacturer's Guide.* Brown Publishing Co., 1949

Hurum, H.J. *A History of the Fish Hook and the Story of Mustad, the Hook Maker.* Adam & Charles Black, Ltd., London, 1977

Leisenring, J.E. & Hidy, F.C. *The Art of Tying the Wet Fly and Fishing the Flymph.* Crown Publishers, Inc. 1971

Leonard, J.E. *Flies.* A.S. Barnes and Company, Inc., 1960

McClane, A.J. *McClane's New Standard Fishing Encyclopedia.* Holt, Rinehart and Winston, revised second edition, 1974

McKim, J.F. *FLYideas.* Monthly column in Western Outdoors Magazine. Western Outdoors Publications, 3197-E Airport Loop Dr., Costa Mesa, CA 92626

Noll, H.J. *Noll Guide to Trout Flies and How to Tie Them.* 1965

Ovington, R. *Basic Fly Fishing & Fly Tying.* Stackpole Books, 1973

Wilson, R. & Parks, R. *Tying and Fishing the West's Best Dry Flies.* F. Amato Publications, 1978

Catalog & Materials Sources

Buz's Fly and Tackle Shop. 219 N. Encina St., Visalia, California 93291 Telephone:(209) 734-1151

Creative Sports Enterprises. 2333 Boulevard Circle, Walnut Creek, California 94595 Telephone: (415) 938-2255

Fly Fisherman's Workshop (Buzz Moffett). 895 Silver Spur Road, Rollings, Hills Est., California 90274 Telephone: (213) 377-8514

Hidden Rod Shop. 2623 Gardenia Ave., Signal Hill, California 90806 Telephone: (213) 427-8060

H.L. Leonard Rod Co. 25 Cottage Street, Midland Park, New Jesey 07432 Telephone: (914) 928-2301

IHS, Inc. (Mustad Fish Hooks Distributor) 964 Lincoln,

Denver, Colorado 80203 Telephone: (303) 832-2044

Kaufmann's Streamborn Fly Shop. Mailing Address: P.O. Box 23032, Portland, Oregon 97223. Business Address: 12963 S.W. Pacific Hwy 99W, Tigard, Oregon 97223 Telephone: (503) 639-6400

Ned Grey's Sierra Tackle. 2615 Honolulu Avenue, Montrose, California 91020 Telephone: (213) 249-1361

Out West Flyfishers (See River Systems)

River Systems (formerly Out West Flyfishers). 2968 Scott Blvd., Santa Clara, California 95050

Rogue River Anglers. 3156 Rogue River Hwy., Gold Hill, Oregon 97525 Telephone: (503) 582-1305

Streamside Anglers. P.O. Box 2158, 501 S. Orange, Missoula, Montana 59806 Telephone: (406) 728-1085

The Fly Line, Inc. 2935 Washington Blvd., Ogden, Utah 84401 Telephone: (801) 394-1812

The Hatch. P.O. Box 5624, Tucson, Arizona 85705 Telephone: (602) 749-3775

The Millpond, Inc. 10893 North Wolfe Rd., Cupertino, California 95014 Telephone: (408) 996-8916

Twin Rivers Tackle Shop. 1206 North River Avenue, Sunbury, Pennsylvania 17801 Telephone: (717) 286-8142

Wright & McGill Co. ("Eagle Claw" Hooks). Denver, Colorado 80216

Sources for "Evazote" and Similar Foamed Products*

Importers and/or Wholesale Fabricators and Distributors:

E-Poxy Industries, Inc. 14 West Shore Street, Ravena, N.Y. 12143 Telephone: (518 756-6193

Rocky Mountain Chemical Company. P.O. Box 2494, Casper, Wyoming 82602 Telephone: (307) 265-3227

United Foam. 172 E. Main St., Georgetown, Massachusetts 01833 Telephone: (617) 352-2200

Wilshire Foam Products, Inc. 1240 E. 230th St., Carson, California 90745 Telephone: (213) 775-3761

"Evazote" Retail Sources Direct and/or Mail Order:

Buz's Fly and Tackle Shop. 219 N. Encina St., Visalia, California 93291 Telephone: (209) 734-1151

Fly Fisherman's Workshop (Buzz Moffett). 895 Silver Spur Road, Rolling Hills Est., California 90274 Telephone: (213) 377-8514

J and J Sales (Mail Order Only). 953 Duar Drive, Concord, California 94518

The Millpond, Inc. 10893 North Wolfe Rd., Cupertino, California 95014 Telephone: (408) 996-8916

Valley Fly Tyer (Mail Order). 15220 Willow, Los Gatos, California 95030

"Plastazote" Retail Sources:

Rogue River Anglers (ask for "Bugazote"). 3156 Rogue River Hwy., Gold Hill, Oregon 97525 Telephone: (503) 582-8916

---

*For other sources, check the phone listing in your area under "Plastics/Foam."

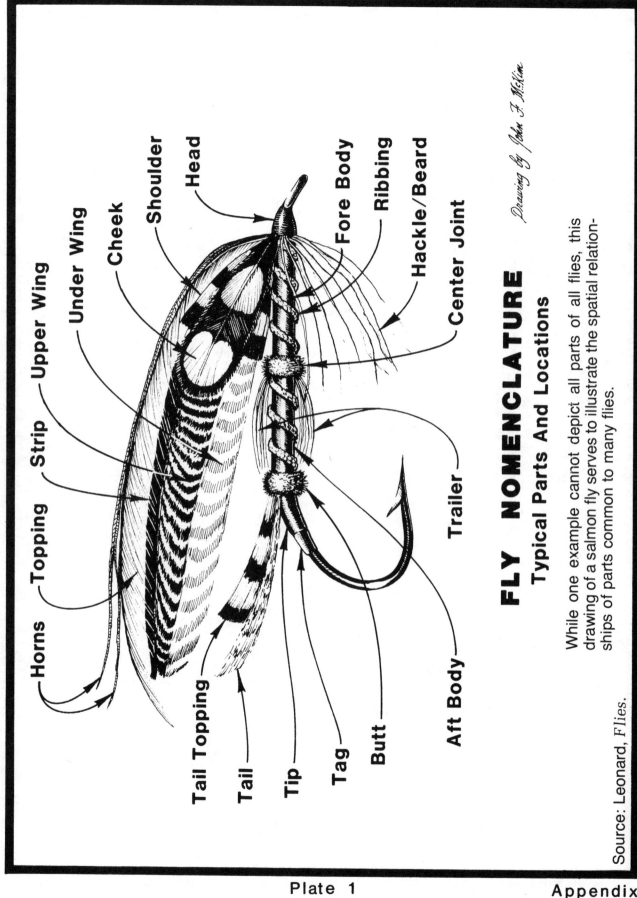

Horns **Topping** **Strip** **Upper Wing** **Under Wing** **Cheek** **Shoulder** **Head** **Fore Body** **Ribbing** **Hackle/Beard** **Center Joint**

Tail Topping **Tail** **Tip** **Tag** **Butt** **Aft Body** **Trailer**

Drawing By John F. McKim

FLY NOMENCLATURE
Typical Parts And Locations

While one example cannot depict all parts of all flies, this drawing of a salmon fly serves to illustrate the spatial relationships of parts common to many flies.

Source: Leonard, *Flies*.

Plate 1

Appendix

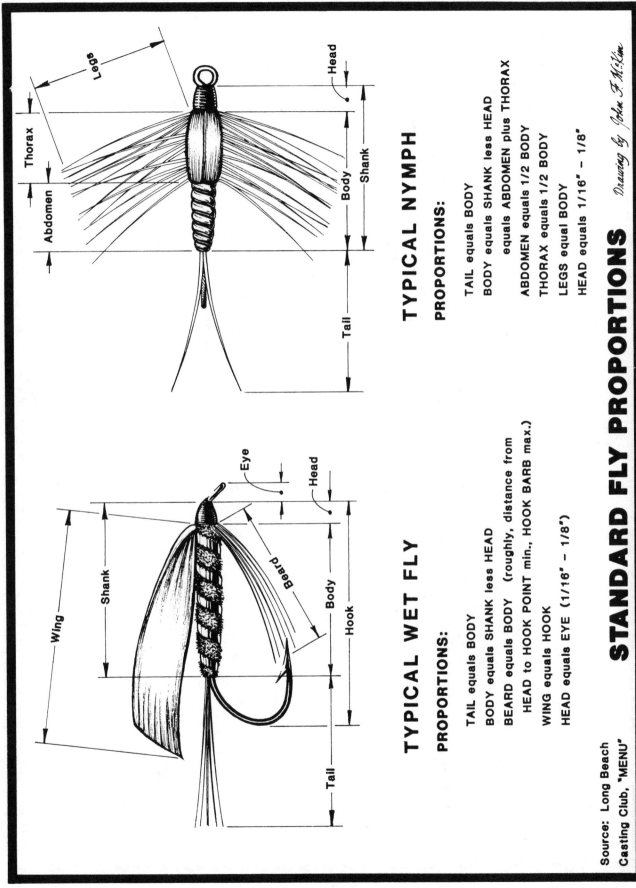

TYPICAL NYMPH

PROPORTIONS:

TAIL equals BODY

BODY equals SHANK less HEAD
   equals ABDOMEN plus THORAX

ABDOMEN equals 1/2 BODY

THORAX equals 1/2 BODY

LEGS equal BODY

HEAD equals 1/16" – 1/8"

Drawing by John F. McKim

TYPICAL WET FLY

PROPORTIONS:

TAIL equals BODY

BODY equals SHANK less HEAD

BEARD equals BODY   (roughly, distance from
   HEAD to HOOK POINT min., HOOK BARB max.)

WING equals HOOK

HEAD equals EYE (1/16" – 1/8")

STANDARD FLY PROPORTIONS

Source: Long Beach
Casting Club, "MENU"

Plate 2   Appendix

137

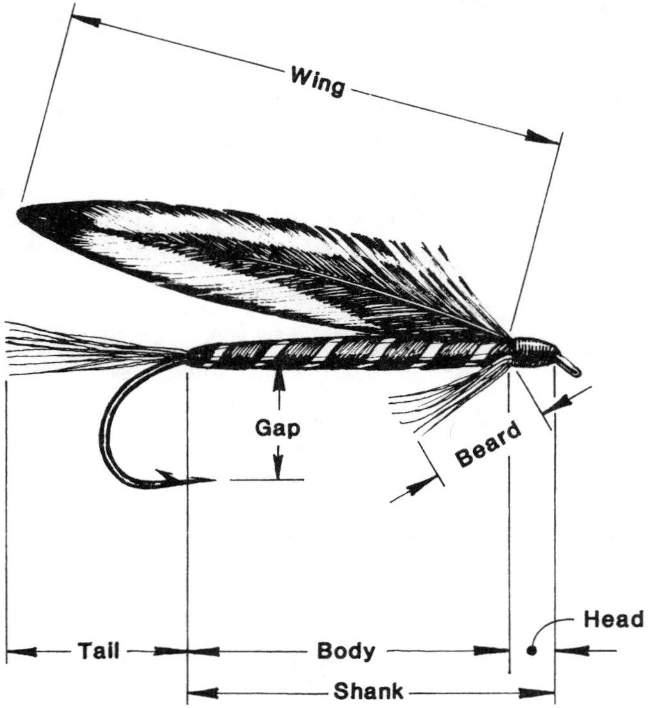

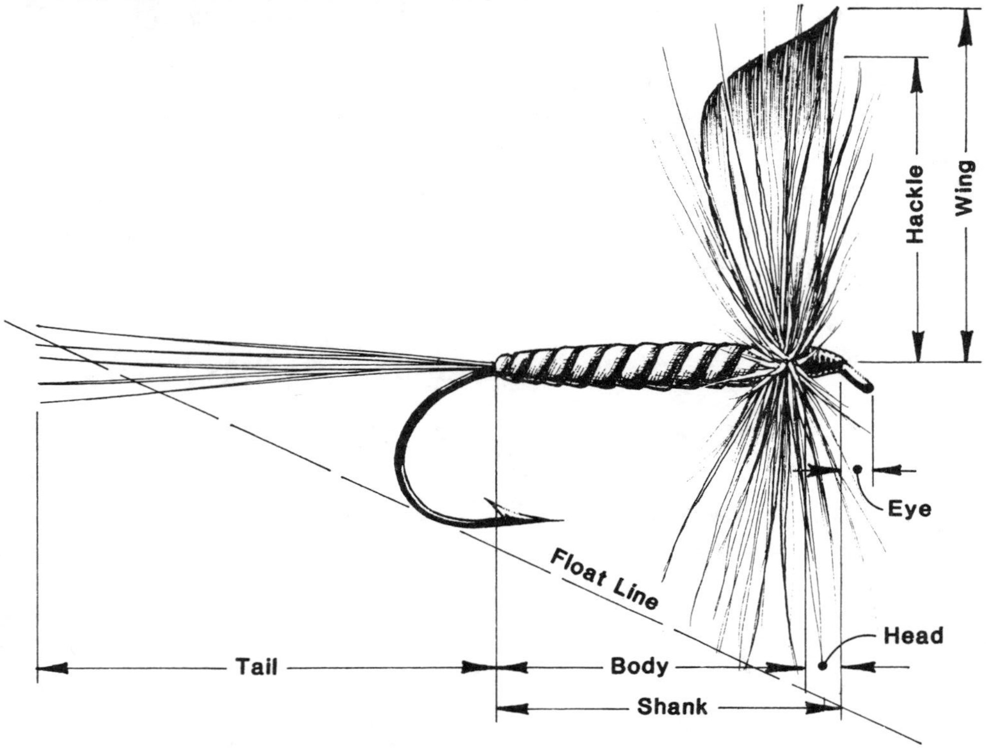

TYPICAL DRY FLY

PROPORTIONS:

TAIL equals 1-1/2 x BODY

BODY equals SHANK less HEAD

WING equals SHANK

HACKLE equals BODY

HEAD equals EYE (1/16" max.)

TYPICAL STREAMER/BUCKTAIL

PROPORTIONS:

TAIL equals 1/2 BODY plus/minus

BODY equals SHANK less HEAD

BEARD equals HOOK GAP

WING equals TAIL plus BODY

HEAD equals 1/8" – 3/16"

STANDARD FLY PROPORTIONS

Drawing by John F. McKim

Source: Long Beach
Casting Club, "MENU"

Plate 3   Appendix

138

TYPICAL FLY WING TYPES

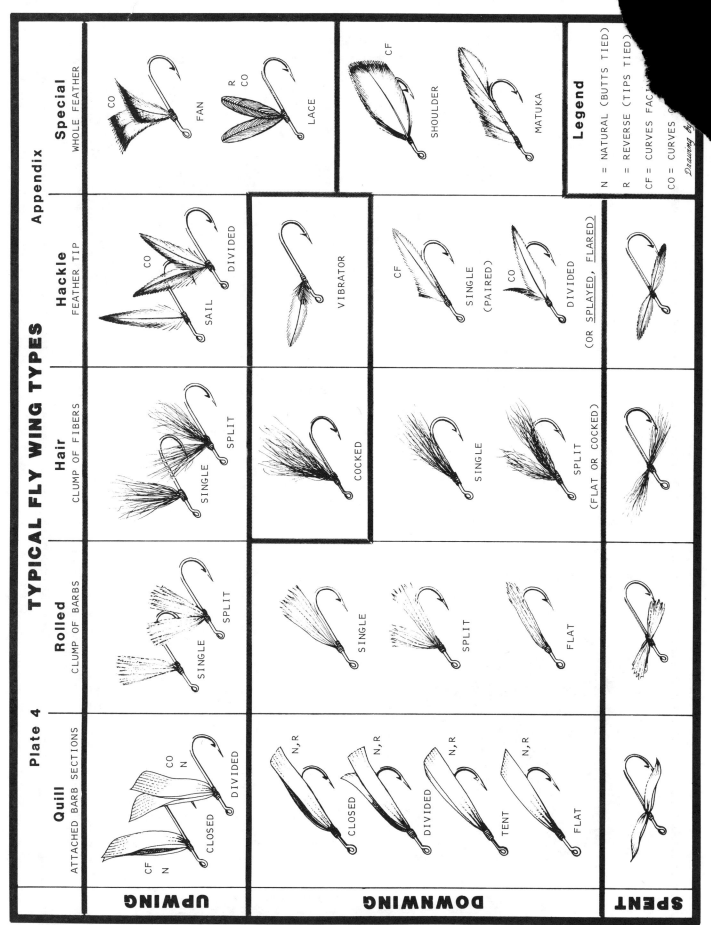

Plate 4

Appendix

Special — WHOLE FEATHER

CO — FAN
R CO — LACE
CF — SHOULDER
MATUKA

Legend

N = NATURAL (BUTTS TIED)

R = REVERSE (TIPS TIED)

CF = CURVES FACING

CO = CURVES O

Drawing by

Hackle — FEATHER TIP

CO — SAIL — DIVIDED
VIBRATOR
CF — SINGLE (PAIRED)
CO — DIVIDED (OR SPLAYED, FLARED)

Hair — CLUMP OF FIBERS

SINGLE — SPLIT
COCKED
SINGLE — SPLIT (FLAT OR COCKED)

Rolled — CLUMP OF BARBS

SINGLE — SPLIT
SINGLE — SPLIT — FLAT

Quill — ATTACHED BARB SECTIONS

CF N — CO N — CLOSED — DIVIDED
N,R CLOSED — N,R DIVIDED — N,R TENT — N,R FLAT

UPWING

DOWNWING

SPENT

Plate 4

Appendix

139

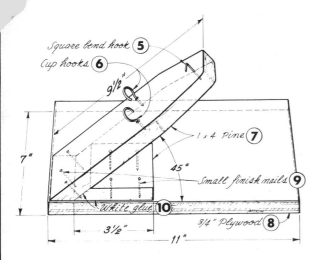

Square bend hook (5)
Cup hooks (6)

9½"

7"

1 x 4 Pine (7)

45°

Small finish nails (9)

White glue (10)

3½"

¾" Plywood (8)

11"

Mounting Stand.

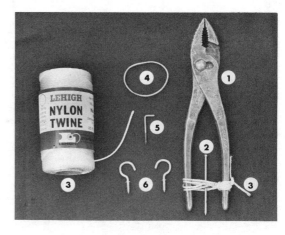

CONSTRUCTION

To fabricate the mounting stand, taper and round off one end of the 1x4 pine (7) and miter saw it at 45 degrees into the two lengths indicated. Apply white glue (10) to each contact surface and install on the plywood base (8) using the finish nails (9). Sand all rough edges smooth and paint the stand if you wish. Install the square bend screw (5) and cup hooks (6) to suit the pair of pliers (1) used.

Install the tightening mechanism as follows: Place a large hook in the jaws of the pliers and wrap the rubber band (4) behind the jaws. The rubber band supplies the constant tension needed to keep the jaws in the normally closed position and the hook loosely in place. Wrap twine (3) loosely around the pliers' handles to form two separate layers of at least three strands each. You will

MATERIALS

One pair of slip-joint pliers (1)
One large finish nail (2)
A length of nylon twine (or equiv.) (3)
One rubber band (4)
One square bend screw (5)
Two cup hooks (6)
One piece 1x4 pine 14" long (7)
One piece 7"x11"x¾" plywood (8)
Small finish nails (9)
White glue (10)

have to determine for yourself how many strands will be required to withstand the pressure without breaking. Wrap the layers together near one handle and tie off with a square knot.

The completed Pliers Vise.

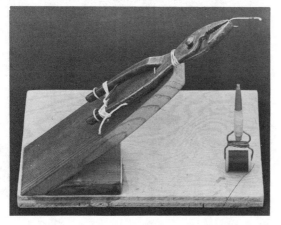

OPERATION

Place a hook between the jaws and orient it to a near 45 degree angle. Insert the large finish nail (2) between the two separate layers of twine and rotate the nail to twist the layers together. This produces a force called torsion which acts to compress the handles, in turn clamping the pliers' jaws. The tighter the twist the greater the pressure. When the hook is sufficiently rigid, place the pliers in the mounting stand as shown. The stand itself will keep the nail from unwinding.

Some types of flat or round nose side-cutting pliers and short needle-nose pliers can also be used; however, long needle-nose pliers usually lack the gripping power at the tip needed to hold even small sized hooks steady enough for fly tying.

HOMEMADE PLIERS VISE

Plate 5   Appendix

140

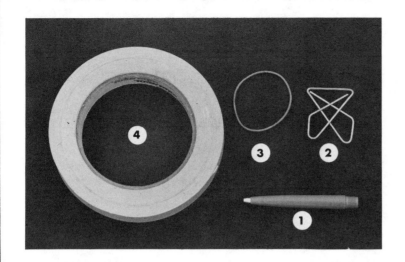

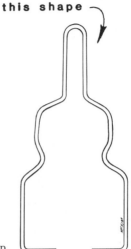

**Bend paper clamp
to approximate
this shape**

Reshaped paper clamp.

MATERIALS

One discarded plastic ballpoint pen, preferably chrome
   tipped **(1)**
One large sized wire paper clamp **(2)**
One rubber band **(3)**
A length of masking tape (or equiv.) **(4)**

CONSTRUCTION

Unscrew the pen (1) and remove the ink tube and spring
assembly. Only the empty writing case will be used.
Straighten the wire paper clamp (2) and bend to the new
shape shown in the drawing. Secure the remodeled
clamp to the empty pen case with tape (4). Place a spool
of tying thread in position with the wire ends inserted
into the spool's hole, then wrap with rubber band (3) in
place to bind the spool. This will create resistance to
thread withdrawal. The amount of resistance — or thread
tension during the tying process — can be adjusted by
increasing or decreasing the wraps of rubber band.

Feed the thread through the empty pen case and you are
ready to tie a fly. Incidentally, if you have trouble feeding
the thread's end through the case, just place the end in
the larger opening and use your mouth to suck it out
through the tip of the bobbin.

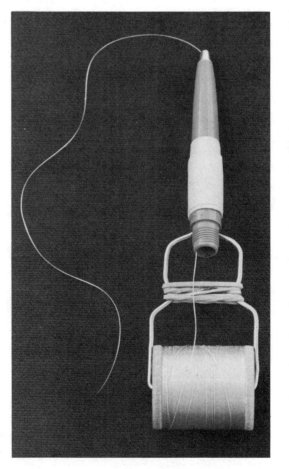

The completed bobbin.

HOMEMADE FLY TYING BOBBIN

Plate 6   Appendix

141

CONSTRUCTION

1. Unscrew the upper and lower halves of the ballpoint pen casing. Remove the innards and discard along with the upper half. You will need only the lower half of the pen casing.

MATERIALS

One discarded ballpoint pen
Ordinary sewing needle 1½″ to 1¾″ long
Masking tape
Paper clip (optional)
Vinyl kitchen magnet (optional)
5-minute 2-part clear epoxy
Tools needed: Sharp knife, pliers

Needle — *Epoxy* — *Shim* — *Ballpoint pen casing*

2. Shim the eyed end of the sewing needle with masking tape wrapped upon itself until the resultant diameter of tape wrapping closely fits within the pen casing's large end. Coat the shim liberally all over with 5-minute epoxy, insert into the pen casing, align straight, coat the outside end of the casing with epoxy then allow to dry.

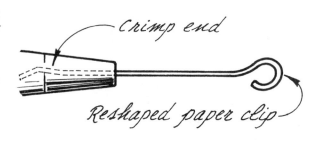

Crimp end — *Reshaped paper clip*

3. For convenient storage on a nail or peg, bend a section of wire paper clip to the shape shown and bond within the pen casing's opposite end with epoxy.

Knife

Vinyl magnet

Trimmed magnet

4. Better still, slice a section from a vinyl kitchen magnet and shape with a knife to fit within the casing's small end.

5. Bond the trimmed magnet in place with epoxy. Be careful not to cover the exposed portion of magnet with epoxy. You will find this feature a valuable aid in retrieving small hooks.

(Dubbing Needle)
HOMEMADE BODKIN

Plate 7   **Appendix**

142

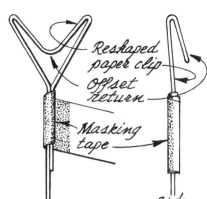

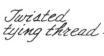

Reshaped
paper clip

Offset
return

Masking
tape

side

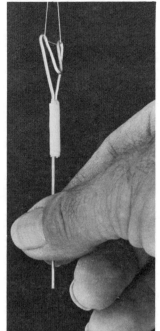

MATERIALS
One large wire paper clip or other wire
of suitable length and diameter
Masking tape
Tools needed: Pair of pliers

*Twisted
tying thread*

CONSTRUCTION
To make this simple, yet effective tool, reshape
the paper clip to the shape shown. Secure the
shorter end alongside the long end with
masking tape. Be sure to provide the offset
return shown.

OPERATION
Place the offset return through the thread loop
to be dubbed. After loop is waxed and dubbed,
twirl the wire shank between thumb and
forefinger to tighten the loop.

HOMEMADE DUBBING TWISTER

MATERIALS
One discarded cigar container
(tube) with slip-on cap, or any
suitable **metal** tubular
container. (Plastic types will
not work; they build up an
electrostatic charge causing the
deer hair to "stick.")
Masking tape

CONSTRUCTION
Wrap an even layer of masking
tape around the tube near the cap
end. Be sure to allow space
between the tube's end and the
inside top of the cap. This will
cause the tips of the tamped hairs
to be revealed when the cap is
removed, making it easier to
remove the aligned hairs.

OPERATION
Trim deer type hair to be aligned
from hide, remove "fuzzy"
underhair and place clumped hairs
in tube, butt first. Slip cap on and
tap the tamper sharply several
times vertically against a hard
surface. Remove cap and hairs, tips
now evened.

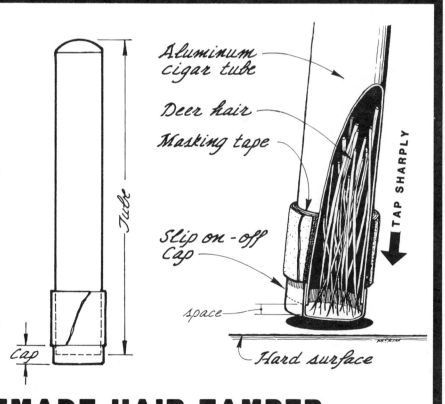

*Aluminum
cigar tube*

Deer hair

Masking tape

*Slip on-off
cap*

TAP SHARPLY

space

Hard surface

Tube

Cap

HOMEMADE HAIR TAMPER

Plate 8   **Appendix**

143

CHAPTER FOUR

ON SALE NOW

VOLUME ONE

Snotlout's dragon Hookfang goes missing and a search party is organized...
Unfortunately, Alvin the Treacherous is also on the hunt for Hookfang...
Who will get to Hookfang first...?

COMING SOON

VOLUME THREE (Available January 6, 2015)

A mysterious trader visits Berk — just as Astrid's dragon, Stormfly, goes missing... The gang's search for Stormfly leads them into frozen dangers and a deadly foe... Plus, in a special short story, Snotlout tries to babysit some baby Monstrous Nightmares!

VOLUME FOUR

(Available March 3, 2015)

VOLUME FIVE

(Available May 5, 2015)

VOLUME SIX

(Available July 7, 2015)

For more information, visit www.titancomics.com